Step Forward

Language for Everyday Life

Multilevel Activity Book

SERIES DIRECTOR
Jayme Adelson-Goldstein

1

Chris Armen Mahdesian

OXFORD
UNIVERSITY PRESS

OXFORD
UNIVERSITY PRESS

198 Madison Avenue
New York, NY 10016 USA

Great Clarendon Street, Oxford OX2 6DP UK

Oxford University Press is a department of the University of Oxford.
It furthers the University's objective of excellence in research,
scholarship, and education by publishing worldwide in

Oxford New York

Auckland Cape Town Dar es Salaam Hong Kong Karachi
Kuala Lumpur Madrid Melbourne Mexico City Nairobi
New Delhi Shanghai Taipei Toronto

With offices in

Argentina Austria Brazil Chile Czech Republic France Greece
Guatemala Hungary Italy Japan Poland Portugal Singapore
South Korea Switzerland Thailand Turkey Ukraine Vietnam

Oxford and Oxford English are registered trademarks of
Oxford University Press

Executive Publisher: Janet Aitchison
Editorial Manager: Stephanie Karras
Editor: Sharon Sargent
Art Director: Maj-Britt Hagsted
Senior Art Editor: Judi deSouter
Art Editor: Justine Eun
Production Manager: Shanta Persaud
Production Controller: Eve Wong

Printed in Hong Kong

10 9 8 7 6 5 4 3 2 1

ISBN-13: 978 0 19 4398244
ISBN-10: 0 19 4398242

Art Credits:
Shawn Banner: 29, 49, 69, 89, 109, 129; Kathy Baxendale: 64; Richard
Deverell: 19, 39, 59, 79, 99, 119; Michael Hortens: 53, 73, 93; Rose Lowry:
34, 74, 94, 114; Karen Minot: 23, 33, 63, 83, 103, 133; Vilma Ortiz-Dillon:
84; Susan Spellman/Gwen Walters: 18, 28, 44, 54, 78, 104, 108, 118; Gary
Torrisi/Gwen Walters: 24, 38, 48, 58, 68, 88, 98, 124, 128, 134.

Photo Credits:
Dennis Kitchen Studio: 1.

A big garland of thanks to the Step
Forward MLAB1 team. To Janet and
Stephanie, for the opportunity to grow.
To Sharon—a wellspring of ideas and
solutions—for careful pruning and picking
off the thorns. Special thanks to Jayme—
my steadfast almanac and trellis, and to
Jane, for planting the seed. I dedicate
this to my parents, Armen & Joy, and to
Christopher, for their unwavering love.
Chris

I take great delight in acknowledging the
Multilevel Activity Book 1 team members,
all of whom performed their assigned roles
brilliantly: Chris Mahdesian—gifted and
inventive writer; Sharon Sargent—witty
and wise facilitator; Maj-Britt Hagsted,
Judi deSouter and Justine Eun—artful
designers: and Stephanie Karras and
Janet Aitchison—gentle timekeepers and
devoted question askers.
Jayme

Acknowledgments

The Publisher and Series Director would like to acknowledge the following individuals for their invaluable input during the development of this series:

Vittoria Abbatte-Maghsoudi Mount Diablo Unified School District, Loma Vista Adult Center, Concord, CA

Karen Abell Durham Technical Community College, Durham, NC

Millicent Alexander Los Angeles Unified School District, Huntington Park-Bell Community Adult School, Los Angeles, CA

Diana Allen Oakton Community College, Skokie, IL

Bethany Bandera Arlington Education and Employment Program, Arlington, VA

Sandra Bergman New York City Department of Education, New York, NY

Chan Bostwick Los Angeles Technology Center, Los Angeles, CA

Diana Brady-Herndon Napa Valley Adult School, Napa, CA

Susan Burlos Baldwin Park Unified School District, Baldwin Park, CA

Carmen Carbajal Mitchell Community College, Statesville, NC

Jose Carmona Daytona Beach Community College, Daytona Beach, FL

Ingrid Caswell Los Angeles Technology Center, Los Angeles, CA

Joyce Clapp Hayward Adult School, Hayward, CA

Beverly deNicola Capistrano Unified School District, San Juan Capistrano, CA

Edward Ende Miami Springs Adult Center, Miami Springs, FL

Gayle Fagan Harris County Department of Education, Houston, TX

Richard Firsten Lindsey Hopkins Technical Education Center, Miami, FL

Elizabeth Fitzgerald Hialeah Adult Center, Hialeah, FL

Mary Ann Florez Arlington Education and Employment Program, Arlington, VA

Leslie Foster Davidson Mitchell Community College, Statesville, NC

Beverly Gandall Santa Ana College School of Continuing Education, Santa Ana, CA

Rodriguez Garner Westchester Community College, Valhalla, NY

Sally Gearhart Santa Rosa Junior College, Santa Rosa, CA

Norma Guzman Baldwin Park Unified School District, Baldwin Park, CA

Lori Howard UC Berkeley, Education Extension, Berkeley, CA

Phillip L. Johnson Santa Ana College Centennial Education Center, Santa Ana, CA

Kelley Keith Mount Diablo Unified School District, Loma Vista Adult Center, Concord, CA

Blanche Kellawon Bronx Community College, Bronx, NY

Keiko Kimura Triton College, River Grove, IL

Jody Kirkwood ABC Adult School, Cerritos, CA

Matthew Kogan Evans Community Adult School, Los Angeles, CA

Laurel Leonard Napa Valley Adult School, Napa, CA

Barbara Linek Illinois Migrant Education Council, Plainfield, IL

Alice Macondray Neighborhood Centers Adult School, Oakland, CA

Ronna Magy Los Angeles Unified School District Central Office, Los Angeles, CA

Jose Marlasca South Area Adult Education, Melbourne, FL

Laura Martin Adult Learning Resource Center, Des Plaines, IL

Judith Martin-Hall Indian River Community College, Fort Pierce, FL

Michael Mason Mount Diablo Unified School District, Loma Vista Adult Center, Concord, CA

Katherine McCaffery Brewster Technical Center, Tampa, FL

Cathleen McCargo Arlington Education and Employment Program, Arlington, VA

Todd McDonald Hillsborough County Public Schools, Tampa, FL

Rita McSorley Northeast Independent School District, San Antonio, TX

Gloria Melendrez Evans Community Adult School, Los Angeles, CA

Vicki Moore El Monte-Rosemead Adult School, El Monte, CA

Meg Morris Mountain View Los Altos Adult Education District, Los Altos, CA

Nieves Novoa LaGuardia Community College, Long Island City, NY

Jo Pamment Haslett Public Schools, East Lansing, MI

Liliana Quijada-Black Irvington Learning Center, Houston, TX

Ellen Quish LaGuardia Community College, Long Island City, NY

Mary Ray Fairfax County Public Schools, Springfield, VA

Tatiana Roganova Hayward Adult School, Hayward, CA

Nancy Rogenscky-Roda Hialeah-Miami Lakes Adult Education and Community Center, Hialeah, FL

Lorraine Romero Houston Community College, Houston, TX

Edilyn Samways The English Center, Miami, FL

Kathy Santopietro Weddel Northern Colorado Literacy Program, Littleton, CO

Dr. G. Santos The English Center, Miami, FL

Fran Schnall City College of New York Literacy Program, New York, NY

Mary Segovia El Monte-Rosemead Adult School, El Monte, CA

Edith Smith City College of San Francisco, San Francisco, CA

Alisa Takeuchi Chapman Education Center, Garden Grove, CA

Leslie Weaver Fairfax County Public Schools, Falls Church, VA

David Wexler Napa Valley Adult School, Napa, CA

Bartley P. Wilson Northeast Independent School District, San Antonio, TX

Emily Wonson Hunter College, New York, NY

Contents

Unit 5 In the Neighborhood

Unit 6 Daily Routines

Unit 7 Shop and Spend

Unit 8 Eating Well

Unit 9 Your Health

Unit 10 Getting the Job

Unit 11 Safety First

Unit 12 Free Time

Introduction to the *Step Forward Multilevel Activity Book 1*

Welcome to the *Step Forward Multilevel Activity Book 1*. In these pages you'll find a wealth of highly interactive activities that require little preparation. All of the activities can be used in numerous ways with a variety of learners. The 110 activities in this book are effective in high-beginning classes as well as in multilevel classes with learners ranging from newcomers to low-intermediate levels.

This book is divided into 12 units that directly correspond to *Step Forward Student Book 1*. Each activity supports and expands upon the student book's lesson objectives, for a complete approach to English language learning.

1 What is the Multilevel Activity Book?

The *Multilevel Activity Book 1* (like the entire *Step Forward* series) is based on research that says adults taught in a learner-centered classroom retain more material for longer periods of time (McCombs and Whistler, 1997; Benson and Voller, 1997). Through its guided and communicative practice opportunities, the *Multilevel Activity Book 1* provides hours of meaningful and fun classroom activities.

2 How do I use these reproducible activities?

The Teaching Notes on pages 3–13 give detailed directions on how to conduct each activity. They also provide multilevel suggestions, guiding you through

1. setting up the activity,
2. modeling/demonstrating the activity, and
3. checking your learners' comprehension of each activity's goal and directions.

Once learners understand how to proceed, they are able to work together to complete the activities. Putting learning into the learners' hands is an important step towards ensuring that they will achieve the lesson objective. Moving away from the front-and-center role frees you to circulate, monitor, facilitate, and gain insight into how well the lesson information was captured. You discover what learners can and can't do well, and adjust your future lesson plans accordingly.

3 What makes these activities multilevel?

One of the key techniques in multilevel instruction is to use materials that can work

The Grid Game in *Multilevel Activity Book 1* allows learners to work at their own level and pace. Higher-level pairs use more complex language to give directions while lower-level pairs use simpler language to perform the same task.

across levels. There are eight activity types in this book. Each one allows you to tailor practice to the learner's abilities, but still have the entire class working on the same basic activity. (See the photo on page one for an example.) Having only ten activity types means that students quickly understand how to do the activities, requiring less teacher intervention and more learner-directed practice. Each activity includes a Keep Going suggestion for a follow-up activity, such as graphing results, discussing answers, or reporting on a task. The ten activity types are described below.

ACTIVITY	GROUPING STRATEGY	DESCRIPTION	CORRELATION TO *Step Forward Student Book 1*
Mixer	Whole Class	Learners get acquainted as they ask and answer questions.	**Pre-Unit: The First Step**
Round Table Label	Small Groups	Learners take turns labeling unit vocabulary in a scene.	**Lesson 1: Vocabulary**
Vocabulary in Action	Pairs	Learners reinforce their understanding of target words and phrases through Total Physical Response.	**Lesson 2: Life stories**
Peer Dictation	Pairs	Partners take turns dictating sentences that reinforce grammar structures while developing their clarification strategies.	**Lesson 3: Grammar**
Role-Play	Small Groups	Learners develop fluency by practicing and expanding upon conversation gambits.	**Lesson 4: Everyday conversation**
Survey	Whole Class	Learners gather classmates' information and graph the results.	**Lesson 5: Real-life reading**
Team Project	Small Groups	Learners work together to complete a project.	**Review and expand**
Picture Cards	Pairs	Partners use flash cards to study the unit's target vocabulary.	**Review and expand**
Grid Game	Pairs	Partners tell each other where to place picture cards on their grids to end up with matching grids.	**Review and expand**
Sentence Maker	Small Groups	Learners use word cards to make as many statements and questions as they can in ten minutes.	**Review and expand**

By having pairs or small groups practice the language required to meet a lesson objective, teachers facilitate learners' use and internalization of the target language. This also provides important opportunities for learners to engage in real-life interaction strategies such as negotiating meaning, checking information, disagreeing, and reaching consensus.

While a pair of running shoes is not required equipment, most multilevel instructors find themselves on the move in the classroom. These highly structured activities support the energetic, communicative, and lively approach to learning that is the hallmark of effective multilevel instruction. The Step Forward Team hopes that you and your learners enjoy these activities.

Please write to us with your comments and questions: **Stepforwardteam.us@oup.com.**

Multilevel Activity Teaching Notes

Teaching Notes for the Mixer

Focus: Students get to know each other by asking and answering questions.
Grouping Strategy: Whole class
Activity Time: 25–30 minutes
Student Book Connection: The First Step

Ready,

1. Select a Mixer activity.

2. Duplicate one activity page for each student.

3. Write the first Mixer question/command on the board.

Set . . .

1. Share the goal of the activity: *You're going to talk to your classmates to learn more about each other.*

2. Have a higher-level volunteer ask you the Mixer question/say the command from the board. Give your answer and then ask the student for his/her answer to the same question.

3. Ask the question/say the command from the board and elicit responses from the class.

4. Distribute an activity page to each student and review the directions.

5. Ask two volunteers to come to the front and model the activity.

6. Check students' comprehension by asking *yes/no* questions. *Do you answer the questions yourself?* [no] *Do you write your name in the chart?* [no]

Go!

1. Set a time limit (five minutes).

2. Have students circulate to complete the activity page. Tell them to sit down when their activity page is complete.

3. Enter the mixer yourself. Students will enjoy your participation and you can check their accuracy.

4. Give students a two-minute warning.

5. Call "time."

Keep Going!

Talk about the results of the mixer using the prompt.

Multilevel Suggestions

Before the Activity:
Pre-Level: Help students read the questions and write their own answers in their notebooks.
On-Level: Have students read the question(s) and write their answers in their notebooks.
Higher-Level: Pair students and have them write three to five new questions on the Mixer topic to add to their activity page.

During the Activity:
On- and higher-level students can stay "in the mix" and help others once their own activity page is complete.

Teaching Notes for the Round Table Label

Focus: Students take turns identifying and labeling the vocabulary depicted in a scene.
Grouping Strategy: Groups of 3–5 students
Activity Time: 20–25 minutes
Student Book Connection: Lesson 1

Ready,

1. Select the Round Table Label activity that corresponds to the unit you are teaching in *Step Forward Student Book 1*.

2. Duplicate one activity page for each group.

3. On the board, post three pictures or draw three objects related to the lesson topic. Draw a line next to each picture. (Students will write the name of the object on the blank line.)

Set . . .

1. Share the goal of the activity: *You're going to work together to label a picture.*

2. Form groups of three to five students.

3. Model the activity. Have one group come forward and take turns passing the chalk and labeling the pictures. Point out that students can label any picture on the board.

4. Once all the pictures are labeled, have the class check the students' spelling in *The Oxford Picture Dictionary* or another dictionary.

5. Distribute one activity page to each group and review the directions.

6. To reinforce the circulation of the activity page within the group, have group members first pass their activity page from student to student, writing their names at the top of the page.

7. Check students' comprehension by asking *yes/no* questions. *Does one person write all the words on the paper?* [no] *Do you pass the paper to the person next to you?* [yes]

Go!

1. Set a time limit (ten minutes). Tell students not to worry about spelling for now. They will check their spelling later.

2. Each student labels one vocabulary item and then passes the sheet to another group member. Students continue taking turns until they've labeled all the items they know.

3. Monitor progress and encourage students to ask their group members for help if they are unsure of a word or its spelling.

4. Call "time" and have students check the spelling of each word in *The Oxford Picture Dictionary* or another dictionary.

Keep Going!

Have students talk about the topic using the discussion prompt on the activity page.

Multilevel Suggestions

For Mixed-Level Groups:
Tell pre-level students that they can say rather than write the words. Instruct on-level and higher-level students to write their pre-level group members' ideas on the activity page.

For Same-Level Groups:
Pre-Level: Give each group of students a list of the words matching the blanks in the picture. Have them complete the activity as outlined above, using the wordlist for help as needed.

On-Level: Have students complete the activity as outlined above.

Higher-Level: Place the picture in the middle of the group and have students pass around a sheet of notebook paper. Have them take turns writing sentences about the picture.

Teaching Notes for Vocabulary in Action

Focus: Students match actions to pictures. Partners then take turns saying and acting out the sentences.
Grouping Strategy: Pairs
Activity Time: 20–30 minutes
Student Book Connection: Lesson 2

Ready,

1. Select the Vocabulary in Action activity that corresponds to the unit you are teaching in *Step Forward Student Book 1*.

2. Duplicate one activity page for each pair.

3. Write out two actions on the right side of the board and illustrate them on the left side of the board. For example, write *Sit down.* and *Stand up.* Draw two stick people: one standing and the other sitting. Number the pictures *1* and *2*.

4. Elicit from students which picture matches which action.

5. Say and demonstrate both actions. Then say the sentences and have students do the actions. Finally, have volunteers say a sentence and you act it out.

Set . . .

1. Share the goal of the activity: *First, you're going to work with a partner and match the pictures and sentences on this page. Then you're going to practice saying the sentences and acting them out.*

2. Pair students and distribute one activity page per pair. Use the example on the page to demonstrate how to do the matching activity.

3. Set a time limit (three minutes) for partners to match the pictures and sentences.

4. Call "time" and check students' accuracy.

5. Have two volunteers demonstrate the next part of the activity.
  • Identify one student as Partner A and the other student as Partner B.
  • Give Partner A the activity page and direct him/her to say the sentences to Partner B.
  • Have Partner B act out the sentences, who acts them out.
  • Have Partner B take the activity sheet and say the sentences to Partner A, who acts them out.

6. Check comprehension by asking *yes/no* questions. *Do you show your partner the paper?* [no] *Can you show your partner what to do?* [yes]

Go!

1. Assign A/B roles to pairs and review the directions.

2. Direct Partner B to act out the sentences Partner A says. Set a time limit (five minutes).

3. Call "time" and have students switch roles. Set a time limit (five minutes).

4. Call "time" and have students take turns giving you the commands. Make mistakes so that they have to correct you.

Keep Going!

Put the pairs into groups. Have a student select a sentence and act it out for the group. The rest of the group guesses which sentence the student is acting out. The first student to guess correctly chooses a new sentence and acts it out for the group.

Multilevel Suggestions

For Mixed-Level Pairs:
Pair higher-level or on-level students with pre-level students. Assign the "acting" role to pre-level students.

For Same-Level Pairs:
Pre-Level: Give each student a copy of the activity page and work with these students as a group to present and practice the commands.

On-Level: Have students complete the activity as outlined above.

Higher-Level: Have students work in groups of three. Assign A, B, and C roles. Have Student A give the command, Student B act out the command, and Student C ask Student A a question such as *What is he/she doing?* or ask Student B *What are you doing?*

Teaching Notes for Peer Dictation

Focus: Student pairs dictate sentences to each other and ask clarification questions to complete the activity page.
Grouping Strategy: Pairs
Activity Time: 15–25 minutes
Student Book Connection: Lesson 3

Ready,

1. Select the Peer Dictation activity that corresponds to the unit you are teaching in *Step Forward Student Book 1.*

2. Duplicate one activity page for each student.

3. On the left side of the board, write a sentence that relates to the topic. Label this side of the board *Partner A.* Label the right side of the board *Partner B.*

4. Familiarize students with the dictation process by asking a volunteer to read the sentence on the left side of the board to you. As you write the sentence on the right side of the board, model one or more clarification strategies: *Can you spell that please?* or *Can you repeat that?*, etc.

Set . . .

1. Share the goal of the activity: *You're going to practice reading, listening to, and writing sentences.*

2. Distribute one activity page per person and review the directions.

3. Pair students. Assign A/B roles to each pair and have them fold their activity pages.

4. Have one volunteer pair model the activity for the class. Ask the pair to come to the front and sit across from each other. Give each partner one of the activity pages. Tell the partners what to do as the class watches and listens.
   • *Fold your papers.*
   • *Partner A, look at the top. Partner B, look at the bottom.*
   • *Partner A, read the first sentence on the page to your partner.*
   • *Partner B, check what you hear.*
   • *Partner B, write the sentence.*

5. When A finishes, have B dictate the first sentence on the bottom half of the sheet to A.

6. Check comprehension by asking *or* questions. *Do you fold or cut the paper?* [fold] *Does Partner A read the A sentences or the B sentences?* [the A sentences]

Go!

1. Set a time limit (five minutes) for A to dictate to B.

2. Call "time" and set a time limit (five minutes) for B to dictate to A.

3. Call "time" and have pairs unfold their papers and check their work.

Keep Going!

Have pairs create four new sentences on the same topic as the Peer Dictation. Have each pair read one of their sentences to the class.

Multilevel Suggestions

For Mixed-Level Pairs:
Pair on-level or higher-level students with pre-level students. Allow pre-level students to either write or to dictate, depending on what they would rather do.

For Same-Level Pairs:
Pre-Level: Provide a simplified version of the peer dictation by whiting out all but a key word or phrase for each item on the activity page and then duplicating it for the students. Conduct the activity as outlined above.
On-Level: Have students complete the activity as outlined above.
Higher-Level: Review the information question words: *who, what, where, when.* Direct students to purposely obscure one of the words in each sentence as they dictate, forcing their partner to clarify before they write. For example, Partner A: *Charles is [cough] ing.* Partner B: *What is Charles doing?*

Teaching Notes for the Role-Play

Focus: Working in groups, students read, choose roles, write the ending, and act out a role-play.
Grouping Strategy: Groups of 3–4 students
Activity Time: 60 minutes
Student Book Connection: Lesson 4

Ready,

1. Select the Role-Play activity that corresponds to the unit you are teaching in *Step Forward Student Book 1.*

2. Duplicate one activity page for each student.

3. Check the "Props" list to determine what items you need to bring to class. Each group will need its own set of props.

4. Check the script to determine what, if any, new vocabulary students will need in order to do the role-play.

Set . . .

1. Share the goal of the activity: *You're going to work in groups and act out different parts in a role-play.*

2. Have students form groups according to the number of characters.

3. Distribute one activity page per person and one set of props per group. Review the directions: *First read the script. Next decide who will play each character. Then write an ending. You must add lines for each character.*

4. Present new vocabulary or review vocabulary as needed.

5. Check comprehension by asking *yes/no* questions. *Do you say all the lines?* [no] *Do you act out your lines?* [yes]

6. Invite two volunteers to the front. Have each pick a line of dialog from the script and act it out for the class.

Go!

1. Set a time limit (ten minutes) for the group to read the script, choose their characters, and finish the role-play.

2. Set a time limit (five minutes), and have the students act out the role-play in their groups.

3. Monitor student progress by walking around and helping with problems such as register or pronunciation (rhythm, stress, and intonation). Encourage pantomime and improvisation.

Keep Going!

Have each group perform their role-play for the class. Ask students, while watching the role-plays, to write the answers to the questions provided in the Keep Going section on the activity page.

Multilevel Suggestions

For Mixed-Level Groups:
Adapt the role-play to include a non-speaking or limited speaking role for pre-level students who are not ready to participate verbally. For example, add a character who only answers *yes* or *no* to questions asked by another character. In large classes, you may want to assign a higher-level student as a "director" for each group.

For Same-Level Groups:
Pre-Level: On the board, write a simplified conversation based on the role-play situation. Help students read and copy the conversation in their notebooks. Then have pairs practice the conversation until they can perform it without the script.

On-Level: Have students complete the activity as outlined above.

Higher-Level: Have students expand the script to create their own version of the role-play using related vocabulary or a similar situation.

Teaching Notes for the Survey

Focus: Students ask and answer classmates' questions and then work individually to record and graph the results.
Grouping Strategy: Individual
Activity Time: 35 minutes
Student Book Connection: Lesson 5

Ready,

1. Select the Survey activity that corresponds to the unit you're teaching in *Step Forward Student Book 1*.

2. Duplicate one activity page for each student.

3. Write the survey question on the board. Draw a simplified chart on the board based on the first row of the survey chart. Then draw a limited bar graph based on the bar graph in the activity.

4. Ask the first survey question and answer it yourself. Chart your response with a check.

5. Ask four students the same question, checking off their responses on the chart as they answer.

6. Remind students that a bar graph is another way to look at information. Transfer the information from the chart onto the bar graph.

Set . . .

1. Share the goal of the activity: *You're going to ask and answer questions about _____ with your classmates. Then you're going to make a bar graph with the information you learn.*

2. Distribute the activity page and review the directions. Check comprehension by asking information questions. *How many questions do you answer?* [all] *How many people do you talk to?* [nine]

3. Have students silently read and respond to the survey questions, marking their response in the column titled "My Answers."

4. Set a time limit (ten minutes).

Go!

1. Direct students to interview nine other students and mark their responses in the chart.

2. Circulate and monitor.

3. Call "time" and have students return to their seats. Ask volunteers to share the responses on their surveys.

4. Remind students how to fill in the bar graphs on their activity page. Set a time limit (five to ten minutes) and ask them to transfer their survey information to the bar graph.

5. Monitor students' progress, making sure that students' bar graphs match the numbers on their chart.

6. Elicit the results of various students' surveys and write the results on the board in sentence form.

Keep Going!

Have students write five sentences about the results of their survey using the sentences on the board as models.

Multilevel Suggestions

During the Survey:
Pair pre-level students with on- and higher-level students. Have the partners work together to survey nine other pairs.

During the Graphing:
Pre-Level: Work with the pre-level group, helping them make a bar graph showing all their survey results.
On-Level and Higher-Level: Have students complete the bar graph as outlined above.

Teaching Notes for the Team Project

Focus: Students work in a group to complete a project-based learning exercise.
Grouping Strategy: Groups of 4–5 students
Activity Time: 60 minutes
Student Book Connection: Review and Expand

Ready,

1. Select the Team Project that corresponds to the unit you're teaching in *Step Forward Student Book 1.*

2. Duplicate one copy of the activity page for each student.

3. Check the materials needed for the project and gather enough for each group.

4. If possible, create a sample of the project students will be doing (e.g., a poster or newsletter).

5. Provide a review of the vocabulary and concepts students will need to complete the project.

Set . . .

1. Share the goal of the activity: *You're going to work in groups to create* [product]. If you have created a sample of what they'll be producing, show it to the students and answer any questions about it.

2. Have students form groups of four or five. Explain the jobs for the activity (see the individual activity page). Allow students to choose their jobs.

3. Ask the Supplier to pick up activity pages for his/her group.

4. Ask the Leaders to read the directions to their groups.

5. Check comprehension by asking *yes/no* questions. *Does one person do all the work?* [no] *Do you make a list of ideas?* [yes]

6. Set a time limit (three to five minutes) for groups to brainstorm answers to the question. The Recorder writes the groups ideas while the Timekeeper watches the clock for the group.

Go!

1. Have students begin to create their projects. Tell students they will have 25–30 minutes to complete their project.

2. Circulate to check students' progress.

3. About twenty minutes into the time period, check with groups to see if they need more time. Extend the time limit by five or ten minutes as needed.

4. Call "time." Have the Reporter from each group tell the class about their project.

Keep Going!

Have students complete the Keep Going activity on the Team Project activity page.

Multilevel Suggestions

For Mixed-Level Groups:
Assign the role of Supplier and Timekeeper to pre-level students. Ask higher-level students to be Leaders and Recorders.

For Same-Level Groups:
Pre-Level: Simplify the project by reducing the amount of reading and writing required. For example, with poster projects, have students label items on posters with single words.

On-Level: Have groups complete the project as outlined above.

Higher-Level: Increase the challenge for students by requiring more writing for the project. For example, have students write a paragraph on how well their group worked together.

Teaching Notes for the Picture Cards

Focus: Students review key vocabulary and grammar using picture cards for flash cards.
Grouping Strategy: Pairs
Activity Time: Various
Student Book Connection: Review and Expand

Ready,

1. Select the Picture Cards that correspond to the unit you're teaching in *Step Forward Student Book 1.*

2. Duplicate one page of Picture Cards for each pair. Have scissors on hand for each pair.

3. Cut apart one of the Picture Card pages to use in the demonstration.

Set . . .

1. Review the directions and the picture card vocabulary as needed.

2. Pair students.

3. Have pairs cut apart the picture cards and write the corresponding word from the word list on the reverse side of each card.

4. Model the activity for the class. Ask a volunteer to hold up a picture card. Say the corresponding word or phrase. Tell the volunteer to look at the back of the card to check if you are correct. Change roles.

5. Share the goal of the activity: *You will use flashcards to practice vocabulary.*

Go!

1. Assign A/B roles.

2. Partner A holds up a picture card. Partner B says the corresponding vocabulary word or phrase. Partner A looks at the reverse side of the card to verify accuracy. Then the students change roles.

3. Allow students to keep their cards for future use.

Keep Going!

Have pairs form groups of four and take turns using the flash cards to see who can name the most words in the shortest time.

Multilevel Suggestions

For Mixed-Level Pairs or Groups:
Be sure each pair or group has at least one on-level or higher-level student who can help guide the pre-level student(s) through the activity.

For Same-Level Pairs or Groups:
Pre-Level: Work with these students separately to review all the pictures. Have students point to or hold up the pictures as first you, then volunteers, say the word or describe the picture.
On-Level: Have students complete the activities as outlined above.
Higher-Level: Allow groups to create their own games with the picture cards. Have a Recorder write the rules. Ask a Reporter from each group to teach the game to the class.

Teaching Notes for the Grid Game

Focus: Students ask and answer questions in order to create matching picture grids.
Grouping Strategy: Pairs
Activity Time: 30 minutes
Student Book Connection: Review and Expand

Ready,

1. Select the Grid Game and Picture Cards that correspond to the unit you are teaching in *Step Forward Student Book 1*.

2. Duplicate one Picture Card page and one Grid Game page for each student and one for you. Have scissors for each pair. Cut apart one of the Picture Card pages to use in the demonstration.

3. Copy the first row of the activity page grid onto the board.

4. Choose three picture cards and draw simplified versions of these cards on three sheets of paper. Put a piece of tape on each paper so it can be attached to the board.

5. Share the goal of the activity: *You're going to play a game to help you practice vocabulary.*

6. Pair students and give each partner a Grid Game page and a Picture Card page. Have students cut apart their picture cards and place them faceup next to their grid. If possible, give each pair a folder to use as a screen between the partners. (See the photo on page 1 as an example.)

Set . . .

1. Ask a volunteer to be your partner. Show your grid page, and tell the student that the grid on the board is his/her "paper." Emphasize that you can not look at each other's "papers." Show the class your three picture cards and give your partner the corresponding hand-drawn pictures.

2. Model the activity.
- Put one picture card on your grid and show the class, but don't show your partner. Then tell your partner where to put the picture card on his/her grid. (If you put the picture of a shirt on the grid square with $30.99 on it, then tell your partner: *The shirt is $30.99.*)
- Encourage the student to clarify. (Student: *$13.99* or *$30.99*? You: *$30.99.*)
- Have your partner tape the correct hand-drawn picture onto the board grid. (The student should tape the hand-drawn shirt picture onto the board in the grid square that says $30.99.) Ask: *Are our papers the same?*

3. Model the activity with the entire class. Circulate and check grids. Then change roles. Have the students tell you where to place your picture cards.

Go!

1. Assign A/B roles to each pair. Remind students not to look at each other's grids.

2. Tell the A students they will start by putting a picture on the grid and telling their partners where to put the same picture on their grids.

3. Set a time limit (ten minutes) and have students work until all the picture cards are on the grids.

4. Have the students compare their grids to see how well they communicated.

5. Have the students switch roles. Set another time limit (ten minutes) and play again.

Keep Going!

Have students write five sentences using the Picture Card and Grid Game vocabulary.

Multilevel Suggestions

For Mixed-Level Pairs:
Assign higher-level students the A role, so that they speak first. Whenever possible, pair students who speak different languages.

For Same-Level Pairs:
Pre-Level: Simplify the grid page by giving each square a number. Have partners give the number of the grid square and the vocabulary word. (Partner A: *One— shirt.* Partner B: *Shirt?* Partner A: *Yes.*)

On-Level: Have pairs complete the activity as outlined above.

Higher-Level: Write a more complex dialog on the board and model it for students to use during the game. A: *Are you looking for a shirt?* B: *Yes, I am.* A: *Here's one for $30.99.* B: *Did you say $13.99?* A: *No, $30.99.* B: *Thanks.*

Teaching Notes for the Sentence Maker

Focus: Students work in small groups to make ten different sentences or questions using word cards.
Grouping Strategy: Groups of 3–4 students
Activity Time: 15–20 minutes
Student Book Connection: Review and Expand

Ready,

1. Select the Sentence Maker activity that corresponds to the unit you're teaching in *Step Forward Student Book 1*.

2. Duplicate one activity page for each group. Have scissors on hand for each group.

3. Draw these six sample "cards" on the board:

CHINA	HE	IS
FROM	?	.

Set . . .

1. Share the goal of the activity: *You're going to work together to make sentences and questions using word cards.*

2. Point out the punctuation cards. Elicit a sentence and a question using the sample cards on the board. Write each on the board.

3. Explain the activity.
- *The group works with the cards to make a sentence or a question.*
- *They dictate the sentence or question to the group's Recorder.*
- *The Recorder writes the sentence and reads it to the group. Then the group repeats the process, making additional sentences and questions.*

4. Check comprehension by asking yes/no questions. *Do you write on the cards?* [no] *Do you make more than one sentence?* [yes]

5. Form groups of three or four students. Distribute one set of cards and a pair of scissors to each group and review the directions.

6. Have each group cut apart the word cards.

Go!

1. Have each group choose a Recorder.

2. Set a time limit (ten minutes) and have groups begin the activity.

3. Monitor and facilitate the students' group work.

4. Call "time." Ask Recorders to tell the number of items they wrote.

Keep Going!

Have each group write two to three of their sentences or questions on the board. Ask the class to give feedback on the accuracy of the sentences.

Multilevel Suggestions

For Mixed-Level Groups:
Create groups that have at least one higher-level student who can serve as the Recorder.

For Same-Level Groups:
Pre-Level: Give pairs a list of sentences and questions that can be made from the cards. Have partners assemble matching sentences with the cards, checking off each sentence on the list as they make it.

On-Level: Have students complete the activity as outlined above.

Higher-Level: Have pairs look at their list of ten sentences/questions they created and write an original corresponding question or sentence for each one.

The First Step

Meet Your Classmates

1. Walk around the room. Interview your classmates.
2. Ask your classmates: *What's your name? Please spell that.*
3. Write the name.

First Letter of Name	Classmates' First Names
A	
B	
C	
D	
E or F	
G	
H	
I or J	
K	
L	
M	
N	
O	
P	
Q or R	
S	
T	
U or V	
W, X, Y, or Z	

KEEP GOING!
What is your teacher's first name? Spell it. What is your teacher's last name? Spell it.

Practice Counts!

1. Walk around the room.

2. Ask your classmates to count or say information.

3. Write the name of your classmate in the chart.

Say	Classmates' Names
Please count to ten.	
Please count from 10 to 20.	
Please count from 20 to 30.	
Please count to 100 by tens.	
Please count the number of students in the class.	
Please say a phone number.	
Please say an address.	

KEEP GOING!

Say the address of your school.

Unit 1 In the Classroom

Our Classroom

1. Work with 3 classmates.

2. Label what you see in the picture.

3. Check your spelling in a dictionary.

KEEP GOING!

Talk about your classroom. What do you see?

© 2006 Oxford University Press • Permission granted to reproduce for classroom use.

Action in the Classroom

1. Work with a partner. Look at the pictures. Match the sentences to the pictures.

2. **Partner A:** Say the sentences.

Partner B: Act out the sentences. Use actions and words.

3. Change roles.

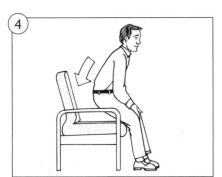
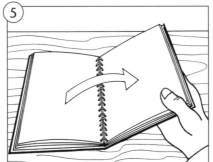
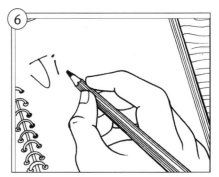
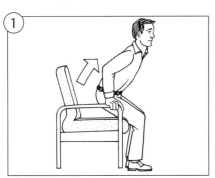

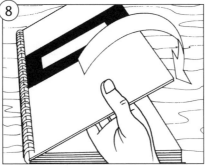

____ Spell your name.

1 Stand up.

____ Sit down.

____ Point to your name.

____ Say your name.

____ Close your notebook.

____ Open your notebook.

____ Write your name.

> **KEEP GOING!**
> Work in a group. Take turns. Act out the sentences. Say what your classmate is doing.

We're Partners

Partner A
• **Read a sentence to Partner B.** • **Answer Partner B's question.** • **Watch Partner B write.**
1. I am a student. 2. I'm not a teacher. 3. You are my classmate. 4. We're partners.
• **Listen to Partner B.** • **Check what you hear. Ask:** *Excuse me?* • **Write the sentence.**
5.
6.
7.
8.

- FOLD HERE -

Partner B
• **Listen to Partner A.** • **Check what you hear. Ask:** *Excuse me?* • **Write the sentence.**
1.
2.
3.
4.
• **Read a sentence to Partner A.** • **Answer Partner A's question.** • **Watch Partner A write.**
5. Mary isn't a teacher. 6. She's a student. 7. She isn't your partner. 8. I'm your partner.

KEEP GOING!

Write 4 sentences about your classmates and school. Talk about your sentences with the class.

We are students. He isn't a teacher.

Making Friends

1. Work with 2 classmates. Say all the lines in the script.

2. Choose your character.

3. Finish the conversation. Write more lines for each character.

4. Practice the lines.

5. Act out the role-play with your group.

Scene	**Characters**	**Props**
At school	• Jamie • Li • Lupe	Books

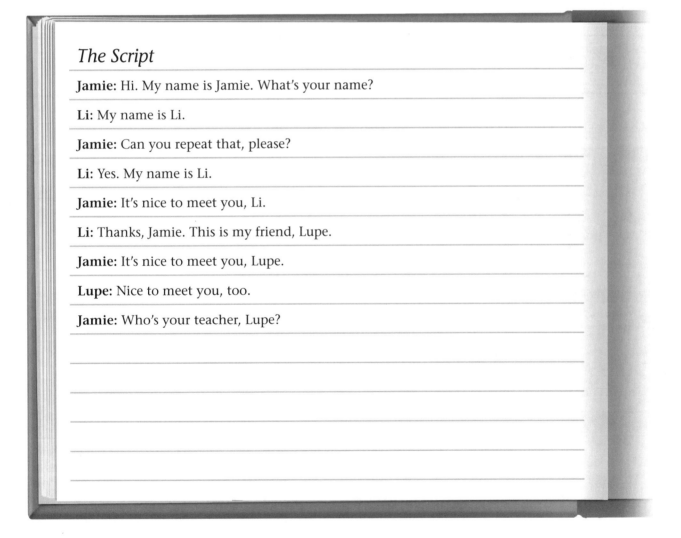

The Script

Jamie: Hi. My name is Jamie. What's your name?

Li: My name is Li.

Jamie: Can you repeat that, please?

Li: Yes. My name is Li.

Jamie: It's nice to meet you, Li.

Li: Thanks, Jamie. This is my friend, Lupe.

Jamie: It's nice to meet you, Lupe.

Lupe: Nice to meet you, too.

Jamie: Who's your teacher, Lupe?

KEEP GOING!

Watch your classmates' role-plays. Write the answers to these questions:
Who is Lupe's teacher? Who is Jamie's teacher?

How Do You Study English?

1. Read the question. Mark your answers with a check (✓).
2. Interview 3–9 classmates. Check your classmates' answers.

How do you study English?	My Answers	My Classmates' Answers								
		1	2	3	4	5	6	7	8	9
I study at home.										
I read in English.										
I speak English at home.										
I listen to the radio in English.										
I ask the teacher or classmates for help.										

3. Use the chart above to complete the bar graph.

Number of Classmates					
10					
9					
8					
7					
6					
5					
4					
3					
2					
1					
	study at home	read in English	speak English at home	listen to the radio in English	ask the teacher or classmates for help

KEEP GOING!

Discuss this information with your class. Write 5 sentences.
4 students listen to English on the radio.

What Are Your Goals?

The Project: Make a poster of your group's goals
Materials: blank paper, magazines, tape or glue, markers, and scissors

1. Work with 3–5 students. Introduce yourself.

2. Choose your job.

> **Leader:** Help your group work together.
> **Timekeeper:** Watch the time.
> **Recorder:** Write the team's ideas.
> **Reporter:** Tell the class about the project.
> **Supplier:** Get the supplies.

3. Talk about answers to this question: Why study English?

> **Timekeeper:** Give the team 5 minutes.
> **Leader:** Ask each person the question.
> **Recorder:** Write the names and answers for each team member.

4. Make the poster.

> **Supplier:** Get the supplies from your teacher.
> **Team:** Draw or cut out the pictures of your goals. Make the poster.
> **Leader:** Help the team think of a title.
> **Recorder:** Write the names under the goals. Write the title on the poster.

5. Show your poster to the class.

> **Reporter:** Tell the class about the poster.
> *These are the goals for our team: English for U.S. citizenship, English for the family,*
> *English for work, and English for school.*

KEEP GOING!
Make a list of the class goals.

    Unit 1 Team Project **23**

Picture Cards

1. Cut apart the picture cards. Use the word list to write the words on the back.

2. Work with a partner.

   Partner A: Show the picture card to your partner.

   Partner B: Say the word.

3. Change roles.

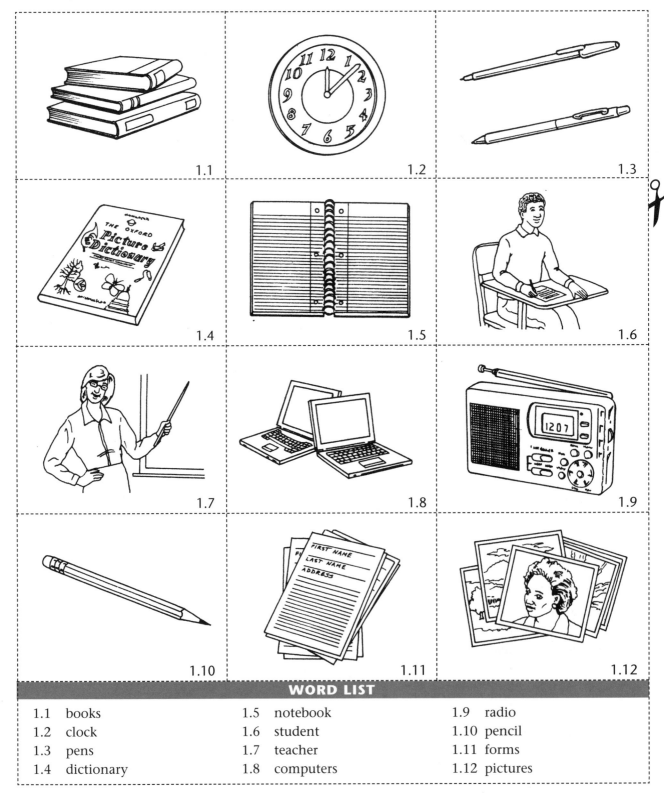

1.1	1.2	1.3
1.4	1.5	1.6
1.7	1.8	1.9
1.10	1.11	1.12

WORD LIST

1.1 books	1.5 notebook	1.9 radio
1.2 clock	1.6 student	1.10 pencil
1.3 pens	1.7 teacher	1.11 forms
1.4 dictionary	1.8 computers	1.12 pictures

Grid Game

1. Cut apart the picture cards from page 24.

2. Work with a partner. Don't show your paper to your partner.

Partner A: Don't show your partner your grid. Put a picture on a square on the grid. Use the picture and the room in the square to make a sentence. Tell your partner the sentence: *The books are in Room 1.*

Partner B: Listen to your partner. Put the picture on the correct square. Check what you hear: *The what?*

3. When your grids are full, look at them. Are they the same?

Yes: change roles. No: try again.

Room 1	Room 2	Room 3
Room 4	Room 5	Room 6
Room 7	Room 8	Room 9
Room 10	Room 11	Room 12

Sentence Maker

1. Work with a group of 3 or 4 students. Cut apart the cards.

2. Choose a Recorder.

3. Use the word cards to make 10 different sentences or questions in 10 minutes.
The Recorder writes the group's sentences and questions.

I	YOU	HE	SHE
IT	THEY	AM	ARE
IS	NOT	A	TEACHER
STUDENT	STUDENTS	BOOK	WHO
MY	YOUR	.	?

Unit 2 My Classmates

What Day Is Today?

1. Work with 3 classmates.

2. Label what you see in the picture.

3. Check your spelling in a dictionary.

KEEP GOING!
Talk about the calendar. What are the months of the year and the days of the week?

Her Favorite Color Is Pink

1. Work with a partner. Look at the pictures. Match the sentences to the pictures.

2. **Partner A:** Say the sentences.

    Partner B: Act out the sentences. Use actions and words.

3. Change roles.

_____ Write your favorite color in your notebook.

_____ Look for your favorite color in the classroom.

__1__ Think of your favorite color.

_____ Name five colors.

_____ Spell your favorite color.

_____ Say your favorite color.

_____ Open your notebook.

_____ Point to your favorite color.

KEEP GOING!

Work in a group. Take turns. Act out the sentences. Say what your classmate is doing.

Yes or No?

Partner A
• **Read a sentence to Partner B.** • **Answer Partner B's question.** • **Watch Partner B write.**
1. Is the teacher tired? 2. Yes, he is. 3. Are the students angry? 4. No, they aren't.
• **Listen to Partner B.** • **Check what you hear. Ask:** *Can you say that again, please?* • **Write the sentence.**
5.
6.
7.
8.

— — — — — — — — — — — — — — — — Fold Here — — — — — — — — — — — — — — — —

Partner B
• **Listen to Partner A.** • **Check what you hear. Ask:** *Can you say that again, please?* • **Write the sentence.**
1.
2.
3.
4.
• **Read a sentence to Partner A.** • **Answer Partner A's question.** • **Watch Partner A write.**
5. Are you from Mexico? 6. Yes, I am. 7. Is your friend from China? 8. No, she's from Korea.

KEEP GOING!

Write 4 *yes/no* questions and answers with *be*. Talk about your sentences with the class.
Are you tired? No, I'm not.

Can You Help Me?

1. Work with 2 classmates. Say all the lines in the script.

2. Choose your character.

3. Finish the conversation. Write more lines for each character.

4. Practice the lines.

5. Act out the role-play with your group.

Scene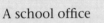

A school office

Characters

- Student 1
- Student 2
- Teacher

Props

- A notebook
- A pen

The Script

Student 1: Can you help me with this form?

Student 2: Sure. What's your last name?

Student 1: My last name is Park.

Student 2: OK. Write *Park* here.

Student 1: OK. What's this question?

Student 2: Hmmm. I'm not sure.

Teacher: I can help you. I'm a teacher.

KEEP GOING!

Watch your classmates' role-plays. Write the answers to these questions: What question does the teacher answer? What is the student's answer?

What's Your Favorite Color?

1. Read the question. Mark your answer with a check (✓).

2. Interview 3–9 classmates. Check your classmates' answers.

What's your favorite color?	My Answer	My Classmates' Answers								
		1	2	3	4	5	6	7	8	9
red										
blue										
yellow										
green										
orange										
purple										
pink										
black										

3. Use the chart above to complete the bar graph.

Number of Classmates								
10								
9								
8								
7								
6								
5								
4								
3								
2								
1								
	red	blue	yellow	green	orange	purple	pink	black

KEEP GOING!

Discuss this information with your class. Write 5 sentences.

Green is the favorite color of 2 students.

All About Us

The Project: Make a poster with the names, countries of birth, birthdays, and favorite colors of your group

Materials: poster or butcher paper, magazines or photos, markers, tape or glue, and scissors

Name: Eduardo
Birthday: July 21st
Favorite color: blue

Name: Helen
Birthday: March 22nd
Favorite color: purple

Name: Joy
Birthday: February 1st
Favorite color: green

1. Work with 3–5 students. Introduce yourself.

2. Choose your job.

> **Leader:** Help your group work together.
> **Timekeeper:** Watch the time.
> **Recorder:** Write the team's ideas.
> **Reporter:** Tell the class about the project.
> **Supplier:** Get the supplies.

3. Talk about the answers to these questions: What's your name? Where are you from? What's your birthday? What's your favorite color?

> **Timekeeper:** Give the team 8 minutes.
> **Leader:** Ask each person the questions.
> **Recorder:** Write the answers for each team member.

4. Make the poster.

> **Supplier:** Get the supplies from your teacher.
> **Team:** Make the poster.
> - Draw a picture or glue a photo of each team member.
> - Draw or glue a picture of where they are from.
> - Label the country.
> - Write their birthday and favorite color.
> **Recorder:** Write the name of each team member and his or her information.

5. Show your project to the class.

> **Reporter:** Tell the class about each group member.
> *This is Joy. Joy is from China. Her birthday is February 1st. Her favorite color is green.*

KEEP GOING!
Who has the same favorite color? Are two or more birthdays in the same month?

Picture Cards

1. Cut apart the picture cards. Use the word list to write the words on the back.

2. Work with a partner.

   Partner A: Show the picture card to your partner.

   Partner B: Say the words.

3. Change roles.

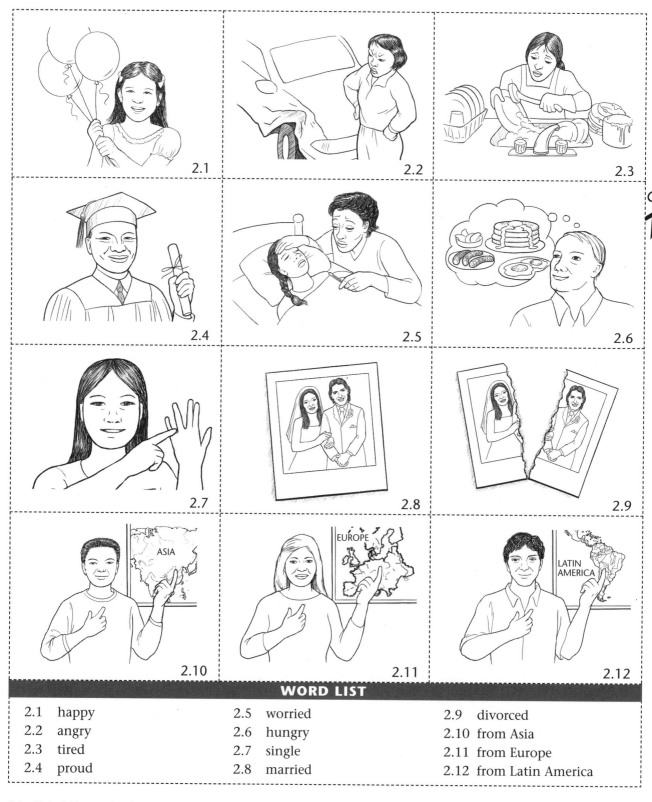

2.1	2.2	2.3
2.4	2.5	2.6
2.7	2.8	2.9
2.10	2.11	2.12

WORD LIST

2.1 happy	2.5 worried	2.9 divorced
2.2 angry	2.6 hungry	2.10 from Asia
2.3 tired	2.7 single	2.11 from Europe
2.4 proud	2.8 married	2.12 from Latin America

Grid Game

1. Cut apart the picture cards from page 34.

2. Work with a partner. Don't show your paper to your partner.

   Partner A: Put a picture on a square on the grid. Use the picture and the name (or names) in the square to make a sentence. Tell your partner the sentence: *Bella is happy.*

   Partner B: Listen to your partner. Put your picture on the person (or people) that Partner A says. Check what you hear: *Who?*

3. When your grids are full, look at them. Are they the same?

   Yes: change roles. No: try again.

Li	Bella	Pedro
Kunkio	Mr. Lee	Neela and Mark
Lan	Ms. Santos	Ray and Nira
Jin	Mary	Minda

Sentence Maker

1. Work with a group of 3 or 4 students. Cut apart the cards.
2. Choose a Recorder.
3. Use the word cards to make 10 different sentences or questions in 10 minutes.
   The Recorder writes the group's sentences and questions.

I	YOU	SHE	HE
WE	THEY	YES	NO
AM	ARE	IS	NOT
AREN'T	ISN'T	HAPPY	HUNGRY
ANGRY	,	.	?

Unit 3 Family and Friends

We're All Here

1. Work with 3 classmates.
2. Label the family members you see in the picture.
3. Check your spelling in a dictionary.

mother

KEEP GOING!

Talk about the different members in a family. What other family members can you name?

Describe the Pictures

1. Work with a partner. Look at the pictures. Match the sentences to the pictures.

2. **Partner A:** Say the sentences.

   Partner B: Act out the sentences. Use actions and words.

3. Change roles.

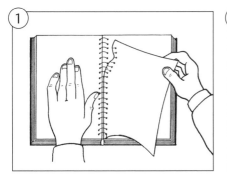 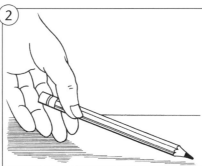 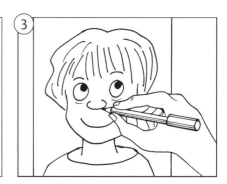

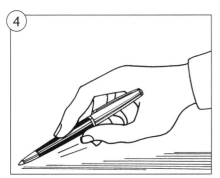  

____ Give the people names.

____ Draw a woman with short gray hair and big eyes.

_1_ Get a piece of paper.

____ Draw a tall man with black hair.

____ Describe your pictures.

____ Show your pictures to your partner.

____ Pick up a pencil.

____ Pick up a black pen.

KEEP GOING!

Work in a group. Take turns. Act out the sentences. Say what your classmate is doing.

We're Family!

Partner A
• **Read a sentence to Partner B.** • **Answer Partner B's question.** • **Watch Partner B write.**
1. Our father's name is Joe. 2. His hair is brown. 3. His sister's name is Alma. 4. Alma's hair is red.
• **Listen to Partner B.** • **Check what you hear. Ask:** *Can you repeat that, please?* • **Write the sentence.**
5.
6.
7.
8.

- - - - - - - - - - - - - - - - - - - FOLD HERE - - - - - - - - - - - - - - - - - - -

Partner B
• **Listen to Partner A.** • **Check what you hear. Ask:** *Can you repeat that, please?* • **Write the sentence.**
1.
2.
3.
4.
• **Read a sentence to Partner A.** • **Answer Partner A's question.** • **Watch Partner A write.**
5. Charlie and Eric are Alma's sons. 6. Charlie's hair is black. 7. Eric's hair is blond. 8. They're our cousins.

KEEP GOING!

Write 4 sentences about your family or friends.
Talk about your sentences with the class.
Asha's hair is brown. Her eyes are green.

Welcome to Our Home

1. Work with 3 classmates. Say all the lines in the script.
2. Choose your character.
3. Finish the conversation. Write more lines for each character.
4. Practice the lines.
5. Act out the role-play with your group.

Scene	Characters	Props
A birthday party at a friend's home	• Guest 1 • Guest 2 • Pat • Family Member	• A box with a ribbon or bow on it • Plastic or paper cups

The Script

Guests 1 and 2: Happy Birthday, Pat! This gift is for you.

Pat: Thank you very much. Thanks for coming to my party.

Family Member: Welcome to our home. Do you want anything to drink?

Guest 1: Yes, please. I'm very thirsty!

Guest 2: Is today your birthday, Pat?

Pat: No, it's tomorrow.

Guest 1: Is that your cousin?

KEEP GOING!

Watch your classmates' role-plays. Write the answers to these questions:
Is that Pat's cousin? What is the gift?

What Color Are Your Eyes?

1. Read the survey question. Mark your answers with a check (✓).

2. Interview 3–9 classmates. Check your classmates' answers.

What color are your eyes?	My Answer	My Classmates' Answers								
		1	2	3	4	5	6	7	8	9
brown										
blue										
green										
black										

3. Use the chart above to complete the bar graph.

Number of Classmates				
10				
9				
8				
7				
6				
5				
4				
3				
2				
1				
	brown	blue	green	black

KEEP GOING!

Discuss this information with your class. Write 5 sentences.

6 students' eyes are brown.

Who Is It?

The Project: Make a guessing game
Materials: index cards or blank paper and markers

Her hair is brown.

Her eyes are brown.

She's from Peru.

She's a mother.

She's a wife.

Her children's names are Carlos and Francisco.

Who is it?

---

1. Work with 3–5 students. Introduce yourself.

2. Choose your job.

> **Leader:** Help your group work together.
> **Timekeeper:** Watch the time.
> **Recorder:** Write the team's ideas.
> **Reporter:** Tell the class about the project.
> **Supplier:** Get the supplies.

3. Talk about these questions for each team member: What color are your eyes?
What color is your hair? Where are you from? Tell us about your family.

> **Timekeeper:** Give the team 8 minutes.
> **Leader:** Ask each person the questions.
> **Recorder:** Write the answers for each team member.

4. Make the game.

> **Supplier:** Get the supplies from your teacher.
> **Team:** Make one card for each team member. Write the name of each
> team member on a separate card. On the other side, write the description
> for the team member. At the bottom, write: *Who is it?*
> **Leader:** Help the team make the cards.

5. Play the game with the class.

> **Team:** Stand together in front of the class.
> **Reporter:** Play the game with the class. Read the description
> for each team member. Ask the class: *Who is it?* Let the class guess.
> Turn the card over to show the name.

> **KEEP GOING!**
> Answer your teacher's questions about your classmates.

Picture Cards

1. Cut apart the picture cards. Use the word list to write the words on the back.

2. Work with a partner.

Partner A: Show the picture card to your partner.

Partner B: Say the word.

3. Change roles.

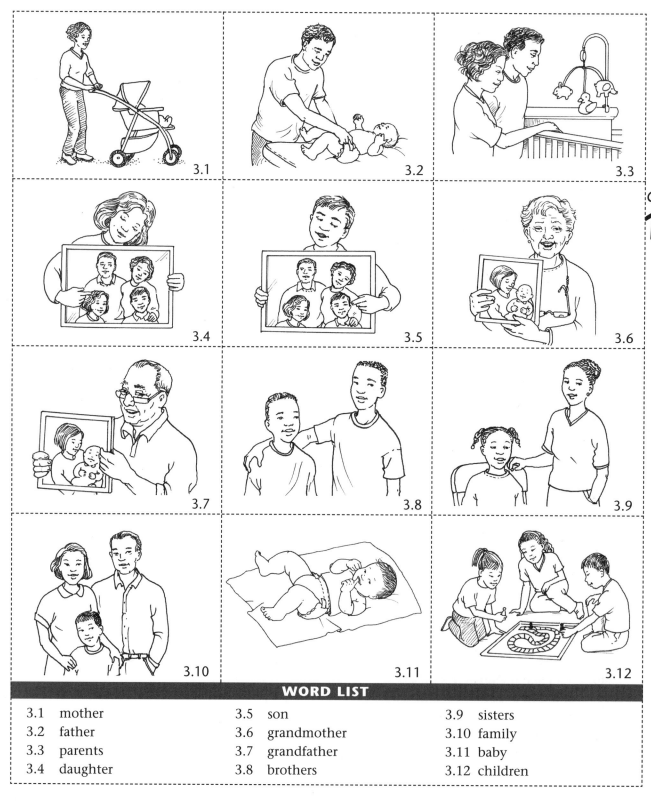

WORD LIST		
3.1 mother	3.5 son	3.9 sisters
3.2 father	3.6 grandmother	3.10 family
3.3 parents	3.7 grandfather	3.11 baby
3.4 daughter	3.8 brothers	3.12 children

Grid Game

1. Cut apart the picture cards from page 44.

2. Work with a partner. Don't show your paper to your partner.

Partner A: Put a picture on a square on the grid. Use the picture and the word in the square to make a sentence. Tell your partner the sentence: *The mother is beautiful.*

Partner B: Listen to your partner. Put your picture on the word that Partner A says. Check what you hear: *Who?*

3. When your grids are full, look at them. Are they the same?

Yes: change roles. No: try again.

tall	short	average
heavy	thin	young
beautiful	attractive	special
fine	good	great

Sentence Maker

1. Work with a group of 3 or 4 students. Cut apart the cards.

2. Choose a Recorder.

3. Use the word cards to make 10 different sentences or questions in 10 minutes.
The Recorder writes the group's sentences and questions.

MY	YOUR	HIS	HER
ITS	OUR	THEIR	EYES
HAIR	FRIEND	SISTER	BROTHER'S
IS	ARE	BROWN	BLUE
TALL	ATTRACTIVE	.	?

Unit 4 At Home

I'm at Home Today

1. Work with 3 classmates.

2. Label what you see in the picture.

3. Check your spelling in a dictionary.

living room

> ## KEEP GOING!
> Talk about the furniture in your home. What's in the living room?
> The kitchen? The bedroom?

There's a Lot to Do!

1. Work with a partner. Look at the pictures. Match the sentences to the pictures.

2. **Partner A:** Say the sentences.

   Partner B: Act out the sentences. Use actions and words.

3. Change roles.

_____ Cook.

_____ Listen to music.

_____ Play a video game.

_____ Sleep.

_____ Wash the car.

__1__ Talk on the phone.

_____ Read a magazine.

_____ Watch TV.

KEEP GOING!

Work in a group. Take turns. Act out the sentences. Say what your classmate is doing.

What's Everybody Doing?

Partner A
• **Read a sentence to Partner B.** • **Answer Partner B's question.** • **Watch Partner B write.**
1. Tim and Jim are sitting in the yard. 2. They're listening to music. 3. My friends and I are talking. 4. We're having a great time.
• **Listen to Partner B.** • **Check what you hear. Ask: *Doing what?*** • **Write the sentence.**
5.
6.
7.
8.

- FOLD HERE -

Partner B
• **Listen to Partner A.** • **Check what you hear. Ask: *Doing what?*** • **Write the sentence.**
1.
2.
3.
4.
• **Read a sentence to Partner A.** • **Answer Partner A's question.** • **Watch Partner A write.**
5. Carlos is cleaning the kitchen. 6. He's mopping the floor. 7. Maria's dusting the furniture. 8. They're doing housework.

KEEP GOING!

Write 4 sentences about what people are doing. Talk about your sentences with your class.
I'm listening to the teacher.

What's the Total?

1. Work with 2 classmates. Say all the lines in the script.

2. Choose your character.

3. Finish the conversation. Write more lines for each character.

4. Practice the lines.

5. Act out the role-play with your group.

Scene

At the kitchen table

Characters

- Roommate 1
- Roommate 2
- Roommate 3

Props

- A phone bill/piece of paper
- An envelope
- A calculator
- A pen or pencil

The Script

Roommate 1: What are you doing?

Roommate 2: We're paying the bills.

Roommate 3: What's the total for the gas bill?

Roommate 2: It's $18.00.

Roommate 3: $80.00!

Roommate 2: No, it's $18.00.

Roommate 3: Oh, that's good.

Roommate 1: When is it due?

KEEP GOING!

Watch your classmates' role-plays. Write the answers to these questions: When is it due? What other bills are they paying?

How Do You Save Money on Utilities?

1. Read the survey question. Mark your answers with a check (✓).

2. Interview 3–9 classmates. Check your classmates' answers.

How do you save money on utilities?	My Answers	My Classmates' Answers								
		1	2	3	4	5	6	7	8	9
turn off the TV										
take short showers										
call long distance after 7 p.m.										
turn off lights										

3. Use the chart above to complete the bar graph.

Number of Classmates				
10				
9				
8				
7				
6				
5				
4				
3				
2				
1				
	turn off the TV	take short showers	call long distance after 7 p.m.	turn off lights

KEEP GOING!

Discuss this information with your class. Write 5 sentences.

5 students take short showers.

Smile! You're on TV!

The Project: Make an ad for a reality TV show about your team living in the same house

Materials: poster or butcher paper, magazines, markers, tape or glue, and scissors

1. Work with 3–5 students. Introduce yourself.

2. Choose your job.

> **Leader:** Help your group work together.
> **Timekeeper:** Watch the time.
> **Recorder:** Write the team's ideas.
> **Reporter:** Tell the class about the project.
> **Supplier:** Get the supplies.

3. Talk about these questions: What room of the house are you in? What are you doing? Are you happy, sad, angry, hungry, proud, or worried?

> **Timekeeper:** Give the team 8 minutes.
> **Leader:** Ask each person the questions.
> **Recorder:** Write the names and answers for each team member.

4. Make the ad.

> **Supplier:** Get the supplies from your teacher.
> **Team:** Cut out or draw pictures of the team members doing their activities and put them in the ad.
> **Leader:** Help the team think of the name for your TV show.
> **Recorder:** Write the captions under each picture.

5. Show your ad to the class.

> **Reporter:** Tell the class about the ad.
> *Miguel is relaxing in the living room. He's happy. Marta's vacuuming in the living room. She's doing all the housework. She's angry.*

> **KEEP GOING!**
> Which team has the best TV show?

Picture Cards

1. Cut apart the picture cards. Use the word list to write the words on the back.
2. Work with a partner.
   Partner A: Show the picture card to your partner.
   Partner B: Say the word.
3. Change roles.

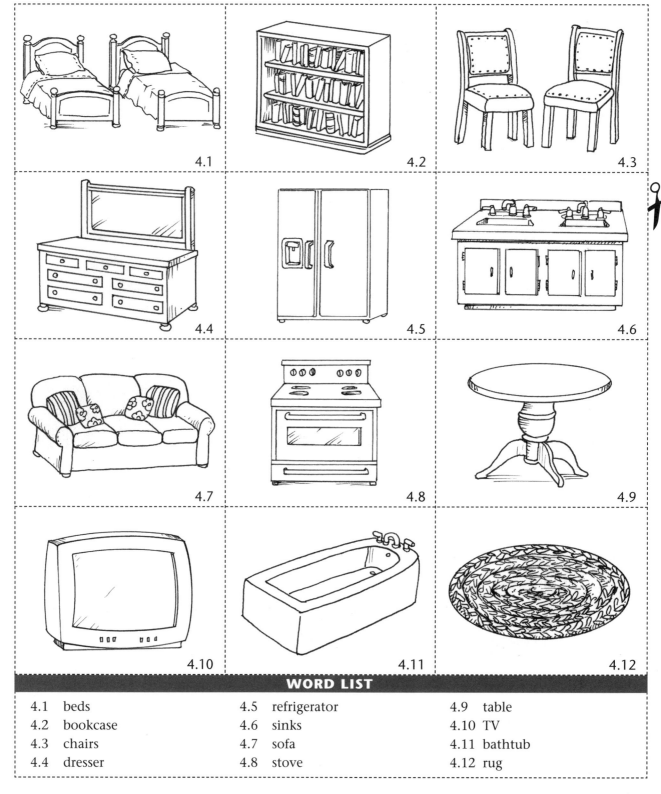

WORD LIST		
4.1 beds	4.5 refrigerator	4.9 table
4.2 bookcase	4.6 sinks	4.10 TV
4.3 chairs	4.7 sofa	4.11 bathtub
4.4 dresser	4.8 stove	4.12 rug

Grid Game

1. Cut apart the picture cards from page 54.

2. Work with a partner. Don't show your paper to your partner.

Partner A: Put a picture on a square on the grid. Use the picture and the color on the grid to make a sentence. Tell your partner the sentence: *The sofa is green.*

Partner B: Listen to your partner. Put your picture on the color that Partner A says. Check what you hear: *What color?*

3. When your grids are full, look at them. Are they the same? Yes: change roles. No: try again.

red	blue	yellow
green	orange	purple
pink	brown	tan
gray	white	black

Sentence Maker

1. Work with a group of 3 or 4 students. Cut apart the cards.

2. Choose a Recorder.

3. Use the word cards to make 10 different sentences or questions in 10 minutes. The Recorder writes the group's sentences and questions.

I	YOU	HE	SHE
WE	THEY	AM	ARE
IS	NOT	ISN'T	AREN'T
COOKING	STUDYING	EATING	PLAYING
DOING	WHAT	.	?

Unit 5 In the Neighborhood

Where's the Supermarket?

1. Work with 3 classmates.

2. Label what you see in the picture.

3. Check your spelling in a dictionary.

KEEP GOING!

Talk about where you live. What places are in your neighborhood?

Here, There, Everywhere

1. Work with a partner. Look at the pictures. Match the sentences to the pictures.

2. **Partner A:** Say the sentences.

  Partner B: Act out the sentences. Use actions and words.

3. Change roles.

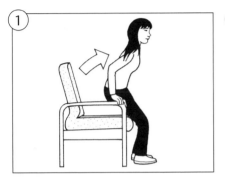

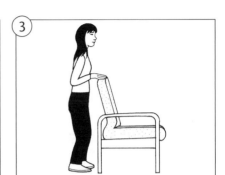
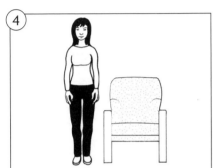
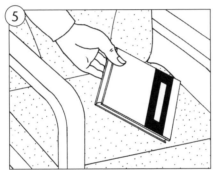

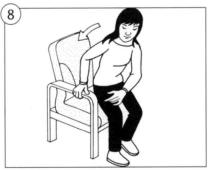

_____ Stand in front of the chair.   _____ Stand next to the chair.

_____ Put the pencil next to the book.   _____ Sit down.

_1_ Stand up.   _____ Stand behind the chair.

_____ Put the book on the chair.   _____ Put the book on the desk.

KEEP GOING!
Work in a group. Take turns. Act out the sentences. Say what your classmate is doing.

Is There a Gas Station on Oak Street?

Partner A
• **Read a sentence to Partner B.** • **Answer Partner B's question.** • **Watch Partner B write.**
1. Is there a gas station on Oak Street? 2. Yes, there is. 3. It's next to the supermarket. 4. It's across from the library.
• **Listen to Partner B.** • **Check what you hear. Say:** *I beg your pardon?* • **Write the sentence.**
5.
6.
7.
8.

- **FOLD HERE** -

Partner B
• **Listen to Partner A.** • **Check what you hear. Say:** *I beg your pardon?* • **Write the sentence.**
1.
2.
3.
4.
• **Read a sentence to Partner A.** • **Answer Partner A's question.** • **Watch Partner A write.**
5. Is there a bus stop on this street? 6. No, there isn't. 7. There's a bus stop on Pine Street. 8. There's a bank across from the bus stop.

KEEP GOING!
Write 4 questions and answers about your school's neighborhood.
Talk about your sentences with your class.
Is there a library across the street? Yes, there is.

Looking for a Good Place to Eat

1. Work with 2 classmates. Say all the lines in the script.

2. Choose your character.

3. Finish the conversation. Write more lines for each character.

4. Practice the lines.

5. Act out the role-play with your group.

Scene	Characters	Props
A street corner	• Friend 1 • Person on the street • Friend 2	A hand-drawn map

The Script

Friend 1: Excuse me. Can you help us?

Person on the street: Sure.

Friend 2: We're looking for a good place to eat.

Friend 1: Is there a restaurant on this street?

Person on the street: No, there isn't.

Friend 2: Where is a good restaurant near here?

KEEP GOING!

Watch your classmates' role-plays. Write the answers to these questions:
Where's the good restaurant? What street is it on?

In Case of Emergency

1. Read the questions. Mark your answers with a check (✓).
2. Interview 3–9 classmates. Check your classmates' answers.

Do you live near a _____?	My Answers	My Classmates' Answers								
		1	2	3	4	5	6	7	8	9
fire station										
police station										
hospital										
clinic										
pharmacy										

3. Use the chart above to complete the bar graph.

Number of Classmates					
10					
9					
8					
7					
6					
5					
4					
3					
2					
1					
	fire station	police station	hospital	clinic	pharmacy

KEEP GOING!

Discuss this information with your class. Write 5 sentences.
2 students live near a hospital.

How Do You Get There from Here?

The Project: Make a map of places around your school
Materials: large paper, markers, tape or glue, and scissors

1. Work with 4–6 students. Introduce yourself.

2. Choose your job.

>**Leader:** Help your group work together.
>**Timekeeper:** Watch the time.
>**Recorder:** Write the team's ideas.
>**Reporter:** Give directions to a place in the neighborhood.
>**Supplier:** Get the supplies.

3. Talk about the answers to this question: What are some places near your school?

>**Timekeeper:** Give the team 5 minutes.
>**Leader:** Ask each person the question.
>**Recorder:** Write the answers.

4. Make the map.

>**Supplier:** Get the supplies from your teacher.
>**Team:** Draw a map of your school's neighborhood.
>**Leader:** Help the team say the directions from the school to one of the places in the neighborhood.
>**Recorder:** Write the directions from the school to one of the places on a different piece of paper.

5. Show your map to the class.

>**Reporter:** Talk about the different places and streets on the map. Then give the directions from the school to a place in the neighborhood.
>*Start at the school. Turn right on Maple Street. Turn left on Third Avenue.*
>*Hamburger Harry's is on the left.*

KEEP GOING!
Have a different group's reporter give directions to a place
on the other group's map.

Picture Cards

1. Cut apart the picture cards. Use the word list to write the words on the back.

2. Work with a partner.

   Partner A: Show the picture card to your partner.

   Partner B: Say the words.

3. Change roles.

WORD LIST		
5.1 post office	5.5 police station	5.9 gas station
5.2 fire department	5.6 bus stop	5.10 library
5.3 pharmacy	5.7 apartment building	5.11 supermarket
5.4 hospital	5.8 bank	5.12 parking lot

Grid Game

1. Cut apart the picture cards from page 64.
2. Work with a partner. Don't show your paper to your partner.
   Partner A: Put a picture on a square on the grid. Use the picture and the phrase on the grid to make a sentence. Tell your partner the sentence: *There's a school on Maple Street.*
   Partner B: Listen to your partner. Put your picture on the location that Partner A says.
   Check what you hear: *Where?*
3. When your grids are full, look at them. Are they the same?
   Yes: change roles. No: try again.

on First Street	on Elm Street	on the corner of Elm Street and Grand Avenue
between here and the next street	across from the movie theater	on Grand Avenue
on Third Street	on Oak Street	in front of the school
next to the park	on Pine Street	on Central Avenue

Sentence Maker

1. Work with a group of 3 or 4 students. Cut apart the cards.

2. Choose a Recorder.

3. Use the word cards to make 10 different sentences or questions in 10 minutes.
The Recorder writes the group's sentences and questions.

IS	THERE	A	SUPERMARKET
BANK	RESTAURANT	IT'S	THE
WHERE	ON	THIS	STREET
NEXT	TO	ACROSS	YES
ISN'T	FROM	.	?

Unit 6 Daily Routines

What Do They Do on Saturdays?

1. Work with 3 classmates.

2. Label the actions you see in the picture.

3. Check your spelling in a dictionary.

relax

What a Job!

1. Work with a partner. Look at the pictures. Match the sentences to the pictures.

2. **Partner A:** Say the sentences.

   Partner B: Act out the sentences. Use actions and words.

3. Change roles.

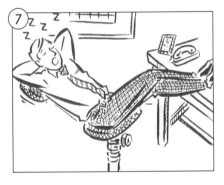

____ Talk on the phone.   ____ Go home.

____ Watch TV.   ____ Eat lunch.

____ Drink coffee.   _1_ Turn on the computer.

____ Sleep.   ____ Listen to music.

KEEP GOING!

Work in a group. Take turns. Act out the sentences. Say what your classmate is doing.

Our Daily Routines

Partner A
• **Read a sentence to Partner B.** • **Answer Partner B's question.** • **Watch Partner B write.**
1. Ed doesn't study English in the morning. 2. He studies English at night. 3. Nancy goes to classes in the afternoon. 4. She doesn't go to school in the evening.
• **Listen to Partner B.** • **Check what you hear. Ask: *What's that?*** • **Write the sentence.**
5.
6.
7.
8.

- FOLD HERE -

Partner B
• **Listen to Partner A.** • **Check what you hear. Ask: *What's that?*** • **Write the sentence.**
1.
2.
3.
4.
• **Read a sentence to Partner A.** • **Answer Partner A's question.** • **Watch Partner A write.**
5. My friends work Monday to Friday. 6. They don't work on Saturday and Sunday. 7. They learn English at work. 8. You and I learn English at school.

KEEP GOING!

Write 4 sentences about a friend or family member's daily routine.
Talk about your sentences with the class.
Grace goes to the library on Tuesday.

It Doesn't Work!

1. Work with 3 classmates. Say all the lines in the script.
2. Choose your character.
3. Finish the conversation. Write more lines for each character.
4. Practice the lines.
5. Act out the role-play with your group.

Scene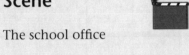

The school office

Characters

- Student 1
- Teacher 1
- Student 2
- Teacher 2

Props

- Papers
- A box with a green button and the word "copier" on it

The Script

Student 1: Pardon me. Do you work here?

Teacher 1: Yes. Do you need help?

Student 2: Yes, we do. This copier doesn't work.

Teacher 1: It doesn't? What's the problem with it?

Student 1: We push this button, but it doesn't copy.

Teacher 1: Hmmm. I'm not sure what the problem is.

Teacher 2: Do you need help with something?

KEEP GOING!

Watch your classmates' role-plays. Write the answers to these questions:
What is the problem with the copier? Who helps the student?

What's Your Favorite Way to Relax?

1. Read the questions. Mark your answers with a check (✓).

2. Interview 3–9 classmates. Check your classmates' answers.

How do you relax?	My Answers	My Classmates' Answers								
		1	2	3	4	5	6	7	8	9
watch TV										
read										
listen to music										
take a walk										
talk with friends or family										

3. Use the chart above to complete the bar graph.

Number of Classmates					
10					
9					
8					
7					
6					
5					
4					
3					
2					
1					
	watch TV	read	listen to music	take a walk	talk with friends or family

KEEP GOING!

Share this information with your class. Write 5 sentences.

3 students watch TV to relax.

What Do You Do in Your Free Time?

The Project: Make a book about what you and your classmates do in your free time
Materials: paper, magazines, markers, tape or glue, and scissors

Carlos plays soccer.   *Maria watches TV.*

1. Work with 4–5 students. Introduce yourself.

2. Choose your job.

> **Leader:** Help your group work together.
> **Timekeeper:** Watch the time.
> **Recorder:** Write the team's ideas.
> **Reporter:** Tell the class about the project.
> **Supplier:** Get the supplies.

3. Talk about the answers to this question: What do you do in your free time?

> **Timekeeper:** Give the team 5 minutes.
> **Leader:** Ask each person the question.
> **Recorder:** Write each person's answers.

4. Make the book.

> **Supplier:** Get the supplies from your teacher.
> **Team:** Fold the papers in half and staple them in the center to make a book. On each page, draw (or cut out and then glue or tape) one picture of what each group member does in his or her free time.
> **Leader:** Help the team think of a title.
> **Recorder:** Write a sentence below each picture. Write the title on the first page.

5. Show your book to the class.

> **Reporter:** Read the book to the class.
> *Carlos plays soccer. Maria watches TV.*

> **KEEP GOING!**
> What's a new activity that you want to try in your free time?

Picture Cards

1. Cut apart the picture cards. Use the word list to write the words on the back.

2. Work with a partner.

   Partner A: Show the picture card to your partner.

   Partner B: Say the words.

3. Change roles.

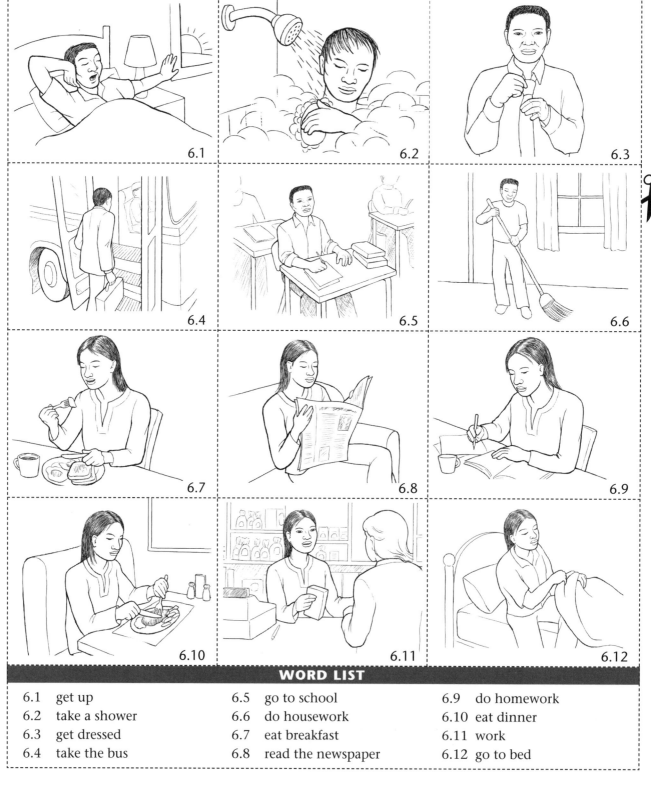

WORD LIST		
6.1 get up	6.5 go to school	6.9 do homework
6.2 take a shower	6.6 do housework	6.10 eat dinner
6.3 get dressed	6.7 eat breakfast	6.11 work
6.4 take the bus	6.8 read the newspaper	6.12 go to bed

Grid Game

1. Cut apart the picture cards from page 74.

2. Work with a partner. Don't show your paper to your partner.

    Partner A: Put a picture on a square on the grid. Use the picture and the time in the square to make a sentence. Tell your partner the sentence: *He takes a shower at 8:15.*

    Partner B: Listen to your partner. Put your picture on the time that Partner A says.

    Check what you hear: *Does what?*

3. When your grids are full, look at them. Are they the same?

    Yes: change roles. No: try again.

6:15 a.m.	6:45 a.m.	7:00 a.m.
8:00 a.m.	8:15 a.m.	10:30 a.m.
5:15 p.m.	6:50 p.m.	7:40 p.m.
8:50 p.m.	9:15 p.m.	10:55 p.m.

Sentence Maker

1. Work with a group of 3 or 4 students. Cut apart the cards.

2. Choose a Recorder.

3. Use the word cards to make 10 different sentences or questions in 10 minutes.
The Recorder writes the group's sentences and questions.

I	YOU	SHE	HE
EAT	EATS	GET UP	GETS UP
USUALLY	DO	DOES	NOT
WHEN	AT	DINNER	BREAKFAST
6:00 A.M.	6:00 P.M.	.	?

Unit 7 Shop and Spend

How Much Is It?

1. Work with 3 classmates.
2. Label what you see in the picture.
3. Check your spelling in a dictionary.

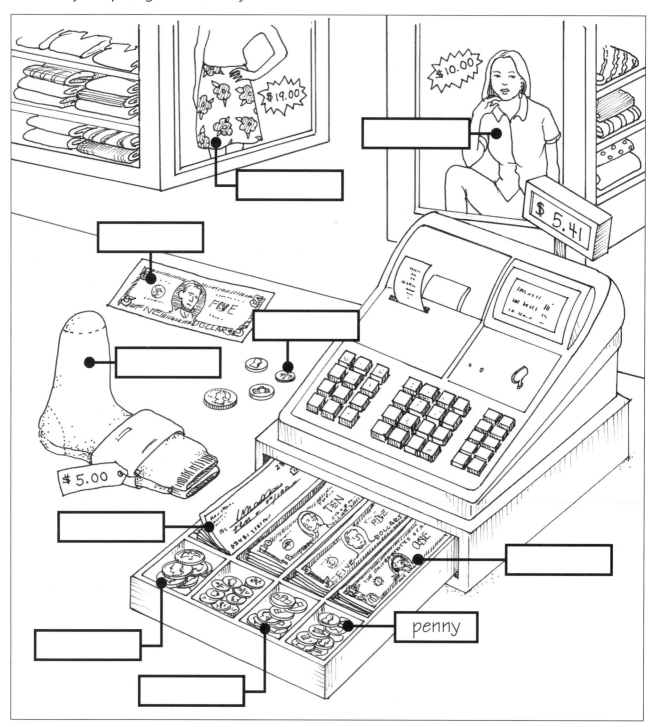

penny

KEEP GOING!
Talk about the prices. How much are the socks, the skirt, and the blouse?

Button Your Sweater

1. Work with a partner. Look at the pictures. Match the sentences to the pictures.

2. **Partner A:** Say the sentences.

   Partner B: Act out the sentences. Use actions and words.

3. Change roles.

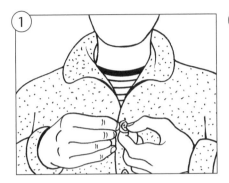

_____ Put on a hat.   _____ Take off your sweater.

_____ Put your scarf in the closet.   _1_ It's cold. Button your sweater.

_____ Hang up your jacket.   _____ Put on a scarf.

_____ It's warm. Take off your hat.   _____ Zip your jacket.

Unit 7 Vocabulary in Action **79**

They're on Sale!

Partner A
• **Read a sentence to Partner B.** • **Answer Partner B's question.** • **Watch Partner B write.**
1. Do you need a new sweater?
2. No, I don't.
3. Does your friend need a new sweater?
4. No, he doesn't.
• **Listen to Partner B.** • **Check what you hear. Ask:** *Can you say that again, please?* • **Write the sentence.**
5.
6.
7.
8.

- Fold Here -

Partner B
• **Listen to Partner A.** • **Check what you hear. Ask:** *Can you say that again, please?* • **Write the sentence.**
1.
2.
3.
4.
• **Read a sentence to Partner A.** • **Answer Partner A's question.** • **Watch Partner A write.**
5. Does this store have suits?
6. No, it doesn't.
7. Does it have jeans?
8. Yes, it does.

KEEP GOING!

Write 4 sentences about things you have, need, or want. Talk about your sentences with the class.
I need new shoes.

Shop Around

1. Work with 2 classmates. Say all the lines in the script.

2. Choose your character.

3. Finish the conversation. Write more lines for each character.

4. Practice the lines.

5. Act out the role-play with your group.

Scene	Characters 	Props
A clothing store	• Friend 1 • Friend 2 • Salesperson	Two shirts

The Script

Friend 1: Look at these shirts. They're beautiful.

Friend 2: They're very expensive.

Friend 1: This one is only $14.00.

Friend 2: $40.00?!!

Friend 1: No! It's $14.00. One-four.

Salesperson: Hello. May I help you?

Friend 2: Do you have this shirt in a medium?

Salesperson: Let me see.

KEEP GOING!

Watch your classmates' role-plays. Write the answers to these questions: Does the salesperson have the shirt in a medium? Are other shirts on sale?

Cash or Credit?

1. Read the question. Mark your answer with a check (✓).
2. Interview 3–9 classmates. Check your classmates' answers.

What's your favorite way to pay?	My Answer	My Classmates' Answers								
		1	2	3	4	5	6	7	8	9
cash										
check										
credit card										
ATM card										

3. Use the chart above to complete the bar graph.

Number of Classmates				
10				
9				
8				
7				
6				
5				
4				
3				
2				
1				
	cash	check	credit card	ATM card

KEEP GOING!

Discuss this information with your class. Write 5 sentences.
2 students like to pay by check.

How to Save Money

The Project: Make a poster that shows different ways to save money

Materials: large paper, magazines, tape or glue, markers, blank paper, and scissors

How to Save Money

Make coffee at home.

Bring your lunch to work.

Call long distance after peak hours.

Cut out and use store coupons.

10% OFF of your n customer

Buy One Breakfast, Get One Free!
Buy one breakfast, get a second of equal or lesser value free.

1. Work with 4–5 students. Introduce yourself.

2. Choose your job.

> **Leader:** Help your group work together.
> **Timekeeper:** Watch the time.
> **Recorder:** Write the team's ideas.
> **Reporter:** Tell the class about the project.
> **Supplier:** Get the supplies.

3. Talk about the answers to this question: What are different ways to save money?

> **Timekeeper:** Give the team 5 minutes.
> **Leader:** Ask each person the question.
> **Recorder:** Write the names and answers for each team member.

4. Make the poster.

> **Supplier:** Get the supplies from your teacher.
> **Team:** Draw or cut out the pictures of your ideas to save money. Make the poster.
> **Leader:** Help the team think of a title.
> **Recorder:** Write the idea under each picture. Write the title on the poster.

5. Show your poster to the class.

> **Reporter:** Read the ideas to the class.
> *We can save money by making coffee at home, bringing our lunch to work,*
> *calling long distance in the evenings after 9 p.m., and using coupons.*

KEEP GOING!
Try a new way to save money for a week. How much money do you save?

Picture Cards

1. Cut apart the picture cards. Use the word list to write the words on the back.

2. Work with a partner.

   Partner A: Show the picture card to your partner.

   Partner B: Say the word.

3. Change roles.

WORD LIST		
7.1 skirt	7.5 shoes	7.9 jacket
7.2 tie	7.6 dress	7.10 T-shirt
7.3 sweater	7.7 socks	7.11 suit
7.4 shirt	7.8 blouse	7.12 jeans

Grid Game

1. Cut apart the picture cards from page 84.

2. Work with a partner. Don't show your paper to your partner.

Partner A: Put a picture on a square on the grid. Use the picture and the price in the square to make a sentence. Tell your partner the sentence: *The pants are $19.99.*

Partner B: Listen to your partner. Put your picture on the price that Partner A says. Check what you hear: *How much?*

3. When your grids are full, look at them. Are they the same? Yes: change roles. No: try again.

$13.99	$14.99	$15.99
$16.99	$17.99	$18.99
$19.99	$50.99	$60.99
$70.99	$80.99	$90.99

Sentence Maker

1. Work with a group of 3 or 4 students. Cut apart the cards.
2. Choose a Recorder.
3. Use the word cards to make 10 different sentences or questions in 10 minutes.
   The Recorder writes the group's sentences and questions.

I	YOU	SHE	HE
WANT	WANTS	NEED	NEEDS
HAVE	HAS	DO	DOES
NOT	A	NEW	SHIRT
SHOES	JEANS	.	?

Unit 8 Eating Well

At the Supermarket

1. Work with 3 classmates.
2. Label what you see in the picture.
3. Check your spelling in a dictionary.

KEEP GOING!

Talk about food shopping. What do you buy at the supermarket?

Enjoy Your Lunch

1. Work with a partner. Look at the pictures. Match the sentences to the pictures.

2. **Partner A:** Say the sentences.

   Partner B: Act out the sentences. Use actions and words.

3. Change roles.

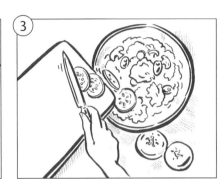

_____ Put the soup in a pot.

_____ Open the can of soup.

_____ Eat the soup and the salad.

_____ Stir the soup.

___1___ Get the vegetables out of the refrigerator.

_____ Make a salad.

_____ Wash the vegetables.

_____ Put the pot on the stove.

KEEP GOING!
Work in a group. Take turns. Act out the sentences. Say what your classmate is doing.

She Doesn't Like to Cook

Partner A
• **Read a sentence to Partner B.** • **Answer Partner B's question.** • **Watch Partner B write.**
1. What does Pam want for dinner? 2. She wants to go to a restaurant. 3. That makes four times this week! 4. She never cooks dinner.
• **Listen to Partner B.** • **Check what you hear. Say: *I'm sorry, what?*** • **Write the sentence.**
5.
6.
7.
8.

- FOLD HERE -

Partner B
• **Listen to Partner A.** • **Check what you hear. Say: *I'm sorry, what?*** • **Write the sentence.**
1.
2.
3.
4.
• **Read a sentence to Partner A.** • **Answer Partner A's question.** • **Watch Partner A write.**
5. How often do you cook at home? 6. I cook twice a day. 7. Do you ever eat at a restaurant? 8. I eat at a restaurant once a week.

KEEP GOING!

Write 4 sentences about how often you do different things. Talk about
your sentences with the class.
I eat with friends once a week.

Let's Order a Pizza

1. Work with 2 classmates. Say all the lines in the script.

2. Choose your character.

3. Finish the conversation. Write more lines for each character.

4. Practice the lines.

5. Act out the role-play with your group.

Scene 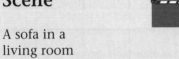	Characters	Props
A sofa in a living room	• Friend 1 • Friend 2 • Friend 3	• A pad of paper • A pen or pencil

The Script

Friend 1: I'm hungry. I want something to eat.

Friend 2: So do I. What do you want to eat?

Friend 3: I don't know. What are you hungry for?

Friend 2: I know. Let's order a pizza!

Friend 3: OK! What toppings do you want?

Friend 1: I like pepperoni. How about you?

KEEP GOING!

Watch your classmates' role-plays. Write the answers to these questions:
What toppings do they order? Do they order anything else?

Eat More Fruit and Vegetables

1. Read the question. Mark your answer with a check (✓).

2. Interview 3–9 classmates. Check your classmates' answers.

How often do you eat fresh fruit and vegetables?	My Answer	My Classmates' Answers								
		1	2	3	4	5	6	7	8	9
more than three times a day										
three times a day										
twice a day										
once a day										
less than once a day										

3. Use the chart above to complete the bar graph.

Number of Classmates					
10					
9					
8					
7					
6					
5					
4					
3					
2					
1					
	more than three times a day	three times a day	twice a day	once a day	less than once a day

KEEP GOING!
Share this information with your class. Write 5 sentences.
3 students eat fresh fruit and vegetables twice a day.

Healthy Choices

The Project: Make a restaurant menu with healthy meal items
Materials: blank paper, magazines, markers, tape or glue, and scissors

Breakfast
Hot Oat Cereal with Raisins
Granola with Yogurt
Whole-wheat Toast

Dinner
Baked Chicken Breast with Vegetables
Grilled Fish with Vegetables
Vegetarian Enchiladas

Lunch
Soup and Salad
Tuna Sandwich
Pasta Salad

Dessert
Frozen Yogurt with Fruit
Melon
Low-fat Muffin

1. Work with 3 or 4 students. Introduce yourself.

2. Choose your job.

> **Leader:** Help your group work together.
> **Timekeeper:** Watch the time.
> **Recorder:** Write the team's ideas.
> **Reporter:** Tell the class about the project.
> **Supplier:** Get the supplies.

3. Talk about the answers to this question: What are healthy things to eat for breakfast, lunch, dinner, and dessert?

> **Timekeeper:** Give the team 5 minutes.
> **Leader:** Ask each person the question.
> **Recorder:** Write the answers for each meal.

4. Make the menu.

> **Supplier:** Get the supplies from your teacher.
> **Team:** Fold the paper in half. Draw or cut out different menu items.
> **Recorder:** Write the healthy foods under each meal (*Breakfast, Lunch, Dinner,* and *Dessert*). Write the name of the restaurant on the front.
> **Leader:** Help the team think of a name for your restaurant.

5. Show your menu to the class.

> **Reporter:** Tell the class about your healthy restaurant menu.
> *For breakfast, order hot oat cereal with raisins. For lunch, order soup and salad.*

KEEP GOING!

Make up a role-play. Order a meal from your menu or another group's menu. What menu items do you want to order for breakfast, lunch, dinner, and dessert?

Picture Cards

1. Cut apart the picture cards. Use the word list to write the words on the back.

2. Work with a partner.

   Partner A: Show the picture card to your partner.

   Partner B: Say the words.

3. Change roles.

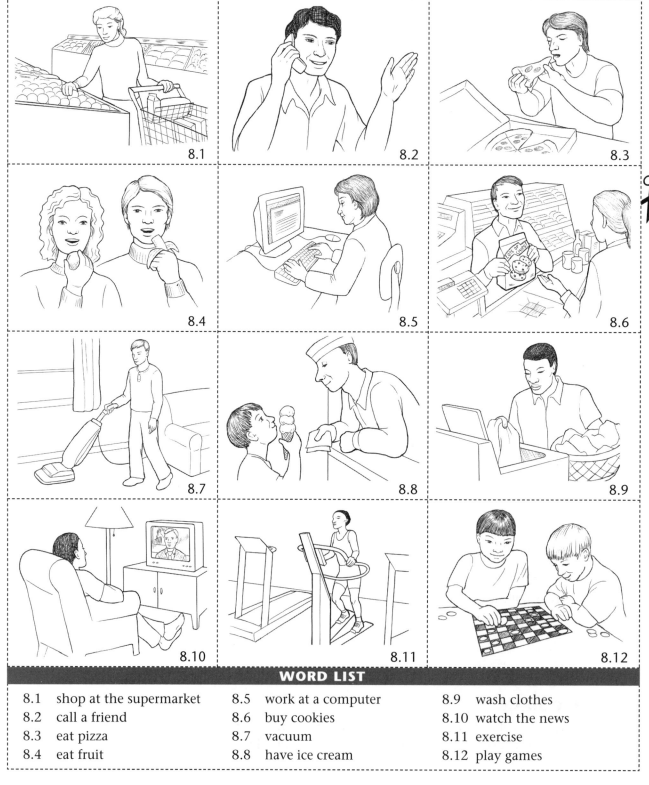

8.1	8.2	8.3
8.4	8.5	8.6
8.7	8.8	8.9
8.10	8.11	8.12

WORD LIST

8.1 shop at the supermarket	8.5 work at a computer	8.9 wash clothes
8.2 call a friend	8.6 buy cookies	8.10 watch the news
8.3 eat pizza	8.7 vacuum	8.11 exercise
8.4 eat fruit	8.8 have ice cream	8.12 play games

Grid Game

1. Cut apart the picture cards from page 94.

2. Work with a partner. Don't show your paper to your partner.

Partner A: Put a picture on a square on the grid. Use the picture and the phrase in the square to make a sentence. Tell your partner the sentence: *He eats pizza once a week.*

Partner B: Listen to your partner. Put your picture on the phrase that Partner A says. Check what you hear: *How often?*

3. When your grids are full, look at them. Are they the same?

Yes: change roles. No: try again.

every day	once a day	twice a day
three times a day	once a week	twice a week
three times a week	five times a week	once a month
twice a month	every Monday	every Saturday

Sentence Maker

1. Work with a group of 3 or 4 students. Cut apart the cards.

2. Choose a Recorder.

3. Use the word cards to make 10 different sentences or questions in 10 minutes.
    The Recorder writes the group's sentences and questions.

I	YOU	SHE	HE
BUY	BUYS	HOW	OFTEN
EAT	EATS	DO	DOES
ONCE	TWICE	FRUIT	DAY
A	WEEK	.	?

Unit 9 Your Health

It's an Emergency!

1. Work with 3 classmates.

2. Label what you see in the picture.

3. Check your spelling in a dictionary.

KEEP GOING!

Talk about the parts of the body. How many different parts can you name?

Time to Visit the Doctor

1. Work with a partner. Look at the pictures. Match the sentences to the pictures.
2. **Partner A:** Say the sentences.
   Partner B: Act out the sentences. Use actions and words.
3. Change roles.

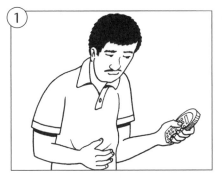

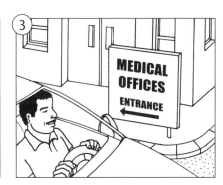

_____ Get a glass of water.

_____ Read a magazine and wait to see the doctor.

_____ Take the medicine.

_____ Drive to the doctor's office.

_____ Buy the medicine at the pharmacy.

__1__ You have a stomachache. Call the doctor's office.

_____ Talk to the doctor.

_____ Make an appointment and write it down.

KEEP GOING!
Work in a group. Take turns. Act out the sentences. Say what your classmate is doing.

Do I Have To?

Partner A
• **Read a sentence to Partner B.** • **Answer Partner B's question.** • **Watch Partner B write.**
1. I have to leave class early today. 2. I have to pick up my daughter. 3. She has an appointment with the dentist. 4. She has a toothache.
• **Listen to Partner B.** • **Check what you hear. Ask:** *Can you repeat that, please?* • **Write the sentence.**
5.
6.
7.
8.

- FOLD HERE -

Partner B
• **Listen to Partner A.** • **Check what you hear. Ask:** *Can you repeat that, please?* • **Write the sentence.**
1.
2.
3.
4.
• **Read a sentence to Partner A.** • **Answer Partner A's question.** • **Watch Partner A write.**
5. Why do we have to leave the party early? 6. Because you have classes in the morning. 7. You have to get up early. 8. Do I have to?

KEEP GOING!

Write 4 sentences about things people *have* or *have to do*. Talk about your sentences with your class.

I have a red book. She has to buy groceries after school today.

Do You Have an Appointment?

1. Work with 2 classmates. Say all the lines in the script.

2. Choose your character.

3. Finish the conversation. Write more lines for each character.

4. Practice the lines.

5. Act out the role-play with your group.

Scene	Characters	Props
A kitchen table	• Friend 1 • Friend 2 • Office Worker	• An appointment card • A telephone

The Script

Friend 1: I have an appointment with my doctor tomorrow.

Friend 2: Oh no! I can't drive you. I have to work.

Friend 1: Well, maybe I can change the appointment.

Friend 2: Good idea! Call the doctor's office.

Office Worker: Hello. This is Dr. Carmen's office.

Friend 1: Yes. I need to change my appointment.

Office Worker: What's your name?

KEEP GOING!

Watch your classmates' role-plays. Write the answers to these questions: What's the new appointment time? Can Friend 2 drive at the new time?

What Do You Do for a Cold?

1. Read the survey question. Mark your answers with a check (✓).

2. Interview 3–9 classmates. Check your classmates' answers.

What do you do for a cold?	My Answers	My Classmates' Answers								
		1	2	3	4	5	6	7	8	9
take over-the-counter medicine										
use a home remedy										
stay at home and rest										
drink fluids										
go to the doctor										

3. Use the chart above to complete the bar graph.

Number of Classmates					
10					
9					
8					
7					
6					
5					
4					
3					
2					
1					
	take over-the-counter medicine	use a home remedy	stay at home and rest	drink fluids	go to the doctor

KEEP GOING!

Discuss this information with your class. Write 5 sentences.

4 students take over-the-counter medicine for a cold.

Make a Prescription Label

The Project: Make a prescription label with directions and warnings
Materials: paper, pens, markers

Chavez, Maria
15 Herman Street
Glenn, New Jersey 07028

SLEEPANITE

Dr. Lee
RX: N1 2345

TAKE 1 TABLET 3 TIMES A DAY.

KEEP IN A COOL, DRY PLACE.

MAY CAUSE DROWSINESS.

---

1. Work with 4–5 students. Introduce yourself.

2. Choose your job.

>**Leader:** Help your group work together.
>**Timekeeper:** Watch the time.
>**Recorder:** Write the team's ideas.
>**Reporter:** Tell the class about the project.
>**Supplier:** Get the supplies.

3. Talk about the answers to these questions: What information is on a prescription? What are some directions for taking medicine? What are some warnings?

>**Timekeeper:** Give the team 5 minutes.
>**Leader:** Ask each person the questions.
>**Recorder:** Write the answers for each person.

4. Make the label.

>**Supplier:** Get the supplies from your teacher.
>**Team:** Make the prescription label.
>• Write the name and address of the "patient" who has to take the prescription.
>• Write the doctor's name and a prescription number.
>• Write and draw the instructions for taking the medication.
>• Write the medicine's name.
>• Write and draw the warnings for the medication.

5. Share your prescription label with the class.

>**Reporter:** Tell the class about the prescription.
>*This is a prescription for Maria Chavez. She must take 1 pill, 3 times every day.*

KEEP GOING!
Look at the other groups' medicine label directions and warnings.
Are there any directions or warnings that are new or that
you don't understand? Ask your classmates what they are.

Picture Cards

1. Cut apart the picture cards. Use the word list to write the words on the back.

2. Work with a partner.

   Partner A: Show the picture card to your partner.

   Partner B: Say the words.

3. Change roles.

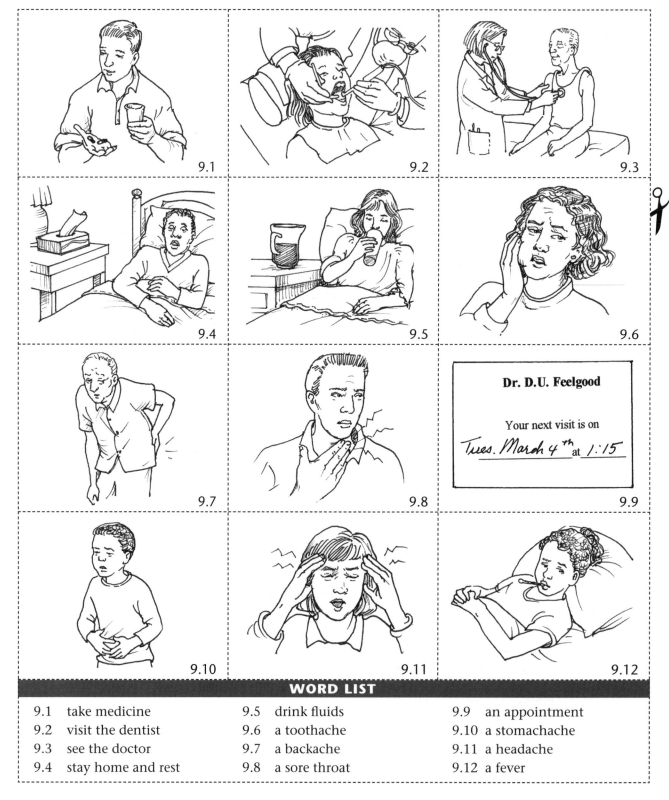

	WORD LIST	
9.1 take medicine	9.5 drink fluids	9.9 an appointment
9.2 visit the dentist	9.6 a toothache	9.10 a stomachache
9.3 see the doctor	9.7 a backache	9.11 a headache
9.4 stay home and rest	9.8 a sore throat	9.12 a fever

Grid Game

1. Cut apart the picture cards from page 104.

2. Work with a partner. Don't show your paper to your partner.
Partner A: Put a picture on a square on the grid. Use the picture and the phrase in the square to make a sentence. Tell your partner the sentence: *Grace has a fever.*
Partner B: Listen to your partner. Put your picture on the phrase that Partner A says. Check what you hear: *Please, tell me that again.*

3. When your grids are full, look at them. Are they the same?
Yes: change roles. No: try again.

Jim has to	Nora has to	Jun has to
He has to	She has to	Ana has
Grace has	Carl has	Mrs. Bostic has
Miguel has	Lee has	Ms. Lake has

Sentence Maker

1. Work with a group of 3 or 4 students. Cut apart the cards.
2. Choose a Recorder.
3. Use the word cards to make 10 different sentences or questions in 10 minutes.
   The Recorder writes the group's sentences and questions.

I	YOU	MY	YOUR
DO	DOES	HAVE	TO
SEE	HURT	HURTS	FEET
FOOT	A	DOCTOR	NOT
REST	HEADACHE	.	?

Unit 10 Getting the Job

Ready to Work

1. Work with 3 classmates.

2. Label what you see in the picture.

3. Check your spelling in a dictionary.

server

KEEP GOING!

Talk about different jobs. What are some different jobs that you can name?

Get a Job

1. Work with a partner. Look at the pictures. Match the sentences to the pictures.

2. **Partner A:** Say the sentences.

   Partner B: Act out the sentences. Use actions and words.

3. Change roles.

_____ Talk about your job skills.

_____ Fill out the application.

_____ Give your application to the manager.

_____ Shake hands with the manager.
      You have the job.

_____ Go on a computer. Print out the application.

_____ Circle a good job ad. Copy the web address.

_____ Put on nice clothes and go to the interview.

__1__ You want a job. Read the help-wanted ads
      in the newspaper.

KEEP GOING!

Work in a group. Take turns. Act out the sentences. Say what your classmate is doing.

I Was Here Yesterday

Partner A
• **Read a sentence to Partner B.** • **Answer Partner B's question.** • **Watch Partner B write.**
1. Was your friend a cook in Poland? 2. Yes, he was. 3. Was he a cook at a restaurant? 4. No, he wasn't.
• **Listen to Partner B.** • **Check what you hear. Ask: *What was that?*** • **Write the sentence.**
5.
6.
7.
8.

- FOLD HERE -

Partner B
• **Listen to Partner A.** • **Check what you hear. Ask: *What was that?*** • **Write the sentence.**
1.
2.
3.
4.
• **Read a sentence to Partner A.** • **Answer Partner A's question.** • **Watch Partner A write.**
5. Were your friends at school yesterday? 6. No, they weren't. 7. Were you at work? 8. No, I was here.

KEEP GOING!
Write 4 sentences about the past with *was* and *were*. Talk about your sentences with your class.
I wasn't at home last night. My friends and I were at a restaurant.

Looking for Work

1. Work with 2 classmates. Say all the lines in the script.
2. Choose your character.
3. Finish the conversation. Write more lines for each character.
4. Practice the lines.
5. Act out the role-play with your group.

Scene	Characters	Props 
A restaurant	• Applicant • Server • Manager	• A pad of paper • A pen or pencil

The Script

Applicant: Excuse me. I'm here to apply for a job. Is the manager here?

Server: The manager is busy right now. Do you need an application?

Applicant: No, I already have one. Here it is.

Server: Oh, you're from Costa Rica. So am I.

Applicant: I was a server in Costa Rica.

Server: So was I. Here comes the manager now.

Manager: Can I help you?

Server: This person is applying for a job.

Manager: That's great. What work experience do you have?

KEEP GOING!

Watch your classmates' role-plays. Write the answers to these questions:
What is the applicant's work experience? Does the applicant get the job?

What Can You Do?

1. Read the survey questions. Mark your answer with a check (✓).

2. Interview 3–9 classmates. Check your classmates' answers.

Can you _____?	My Answers	My Classmates' Answers								
		1	2	3	4	5	6	7	8	9
cook										
fix cars										
use a photocopier										
take care of children										
take care of plants										
serve food										

3. Use the chart above to complete the bar graph.

Number of Classmates						
10						
9						
8						
7						
6						
5						
4						
3						
2						
1						
	cook	fix cars	use a photocopier	take care of children	take care of plants	serve food

KEEP GOING!

Discuss this information with your class. Write 5 sentences.

2 students can use a photocopier.

Help Wanted

The Project: Write a help-wanted ad for a job
Materials: paper, marker, pen, or pencil, or use a word processing program

> HELP WANTED
> Server
> M to F, 7 a.m. to 1 p.m.
> Part-time, 1 yr. Exp. Nec.
> $8/hr. + Tips

1. Work with 4–5 students. Introduce yourself.

2. Choose your job.

> **Leader:** Help your group work together.
> **Timekeeper:** Watch the time.
> **Recorder:** Write the team's ideas.
> **Reporter:** Tell the class about the project.
> **Supplier:** Get the supplies.

3. Choose 1 job. Talk about the answers to this question: What are the usual days, hours, experience needed, and pay for this job?

> **Timekeeper:** Give the team 5 minutes.
> **Leader:** Ask each person the questions.
> **Recorder:** Write the names and answers for each team member.

4. Make the help-wanted ad.

> **Supplier:** Get the supplies from your teacher.
> **Recorder:** Make the help-wanted ad. List the hours, pay, and experience needed for the job.

5. Share your help-wanted ad with the class.

> **Reporter:** Read the ad to the class.
> *Our ad is for a server. It is part-time, Monday to Friday. You need 1 year of experience at another restaurant. It pays $8 an hour plus tips.*

> **KEEP GOING!**
> Write a help-wanted ad for your dream job.

Picture Cards

1. Cut apart the picture cards. Use the word list to write the words on the back.

2. Work with a partner.

Partner A: Show the picture card to your partner.

Partner B: Say the words.

3. Change roles.

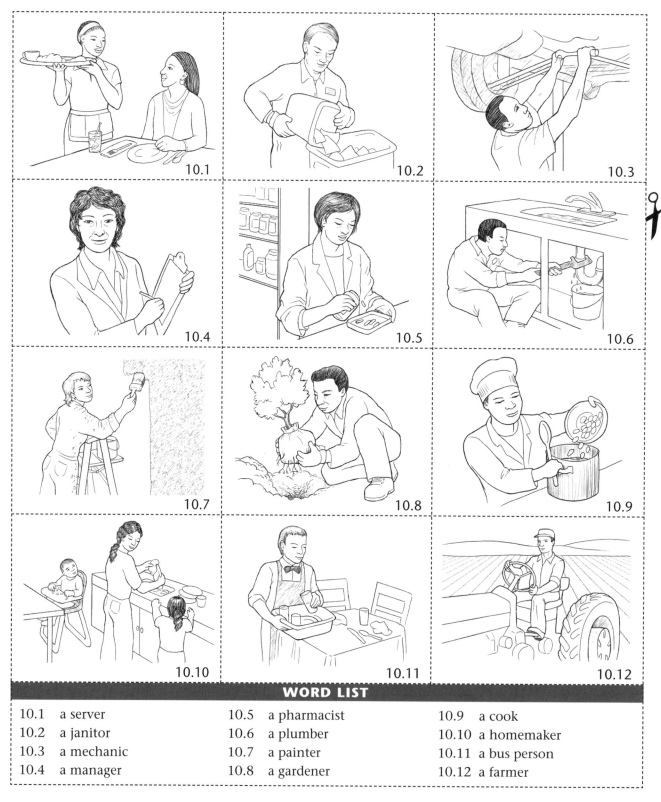

	WORD LIST	
10.1 a server	10.5 a pharmacist	10.9 a cook
10.2 a janitor	10.6 a plumber	10.10 a homemaker
10.3 a mechanic	10.7 a painter	10.11 a bus person
10.4 a manager	10.8 a gardener	10.12 a farmer

Grid Game

1. Cut apart the picture cards from page 114.

2. Work with a partner. Don't show your paper to your partner.

Partner A: Put a picture on a square on the grid. Use the picture and the time period in the square to make a sentence. Tell your partner the sentence: *He was a bus person for 2 years.*

Partner B: Listen to your partner. Put your picture on the time period that Partner A says. Check what you hear: *How long?*

3. When your grids are full, look at them. Are they the same?

Yes: change roles. No: try again.

3 months	6 months	9 months
1 year	1½ years	2 years
2½ years	3 years	5 years
5½ years	7 years	10 years

Sentence Maker

1. Work with a group of 3 or 4 students. Cut apart the cards.

2. Choose a Recorder.

3. Use the word cards to make 10 different sentences or questions in 10 minutes.
    The Recorder writes the group's sentences and questions.

I	YOU	SHE	HE
WAS	WERE	CAN	NOT
WORK	DRIVE	COOK	MANAGER
GARDENER	MECHANIC	SCHOOL	HOME
AT	A	.	?

Unit 11 Safety First

Be Careful!

1. Work with 3 classmates.
2. Label what you see in the picture.
3. Check your spelling in a dictionary.

KEEP GOING!
Talk about different traffic signs. What are some traffic signs you see around your school?

Drive Safely!

1. Work with a partner. Look at the pictures. Match the sentences to the pictures.

2. **Partner A:** Say the sentences.

　　Partner B: Act out the sentences. Use actions and words.

3. Change roles.

____ You're lost. Drive into a gas station and ask for directions.

____ Put on your seatbelt.

____ Watch out for people on the street.

____ You're finally there! Park your car and get out.

_1_ You want to visit your friend. Check your tires.

____ Write down the directions.

____ Stop at the stop sign. Look both ways.

____ Get in the car and lock the door.

KEEP GOING!

Work in a group. Take turns. Act out the sentences. Say what your classmate is doing.

Should I or Shouldn't I?

Partner A
• **Read a sentence to Partner B.** • **Answer Partner B's question.** • **Watch Partner B write.**
1. Should I park my car here? 2. No, you shouldn't. 3. Where should I park? 4. You should park in a parking lot.
• **Listen to Partner B.** • **Check what you hear. Ask:** *Can you say that again, please?* • **Write the sentence.**
5.
6.
7.
8.

- FOLD HERE -

Partner B
• **Listen to Partner A.** • **Check what you hear. Ask:** *Can you say that again, please?* • **Write the sentence.**
1.
2.
3.
4.
• **Read a sentence to Partner A.** • **Answer Partner A's question.** • **Watch Partner A write.**
5. Should I use my cell phone in the classroom? 6. No, you shouldn't. 7. Should I leave to call my friend? 8. No, you should pay attention to the lesson!

KEEP GOING!
Write 4 sentences about different things people should or shouldn't do.
Talk about your sentences with your class.
I should study more. You shouldn't park your car at a bus stop.

There's a Fire!

1. Work with 2 classmates. Say all the lines in the script.

2. Choose your character.

3. Finish the conversation. Write more lines for each character.

4. Practice the lines.

5. Act out the role-play with your group.

Scene	Characters	Props
A street	• Person 1 • Person 2 • 911 Operator	• A cell phone • A telephone

The Script

Person 1: That building is on fire! What should we do?

Person 2: We should call 911. This is an emergency!

Person 1: You're right! Do you have your cell phone?

Person 2: Yes, it's right here.

911 Operator: 911. What's your emergency?

Person 1: There's a building on fire!

911 Operator: What's the address?

KEEP GOING!

Watch your classmates' role-plays. Write the answers to these questions:
What's the address? Was anyone hurt?

How Safe Are You?

1. Read the survey questions. Mark your answers with a check (✓).
2. Interview 3–9 classmates. Check your classmates' answers.

How safe are you? Do you _____?	My Answers	My Classmates' Answers								
		1	2	3	4	5	6	7	8	9
wear a seatbelt										
pull over to use a cell phone										
drive the speed limit										
walk with friends at night										
check your smoke detectors										

3. Use the chart above to complete the bar graph.

Number of Classmates					
10					
9					
8					
7					
6					
5					
4					
3					
2					
1					
	wear a seatbelt	pull over to use a cell phone	drive the speed limit	walk with friends at night	check your smoke detectors

KEEP GOING!

Discuss this information with your class. Write 5 sentences.

3 students wear a seatbelt.

Read the Traffic Signs!

The Project: Make a pamphlet of traffic signs
Materials: blank paper, colored construction paper, scissors, tape or glue, and markers

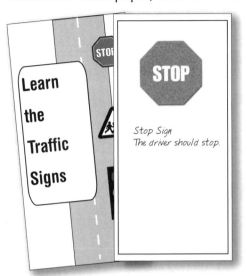

1. Work with 4–5 students. Introduce yourself.

2. Choose your job.

> **Leader:** Help your group work together.
> **Timekeeper:** Watch the time.
> **Recorder:** Write the team's ideas.
> **Reporter:** Tell the class about the project.
> **Supplier:** Get the supplies.

3. Talk about the answers to these questions: What are some different traffic signs?
What does the driver have to do?

> **Timekeeper:** Give the team 5 minutes.
> **Leader:** Ask each person the questions.
> **Recorder:** Write the answers for each team member.

4. Make the pamphlet.

> **Supplier:** Get the supplies from your teacher.
> **Team:** Fold the papers in half and staple them in the center. Draw or cut
> out the traffic signs. Put one traffic sign on each page of the pamphlet.
> **Leader:** Help the team think of a title for the pamphlet.
> **Recorder:** Under each traffic sign, write what the sign is and what the
> driver has to do. Write the title on the front of the pamphlet.

5. Show your pamphlet to the class.

> **Reporter:** Tell the class about the pamphlet.
> *This is a stop sign. The driver should stop.*

KEEP GOING!
Write a list of things a person should or shouldn't do to be a safe driver.

Picture Cards

1. Cut apart the picture cards. Use the word list to write the words on the back.
2. Work with a partner.
   Partner A: Show the picture card to your partner.
   Partner B: Say the words.
3. Change roles.

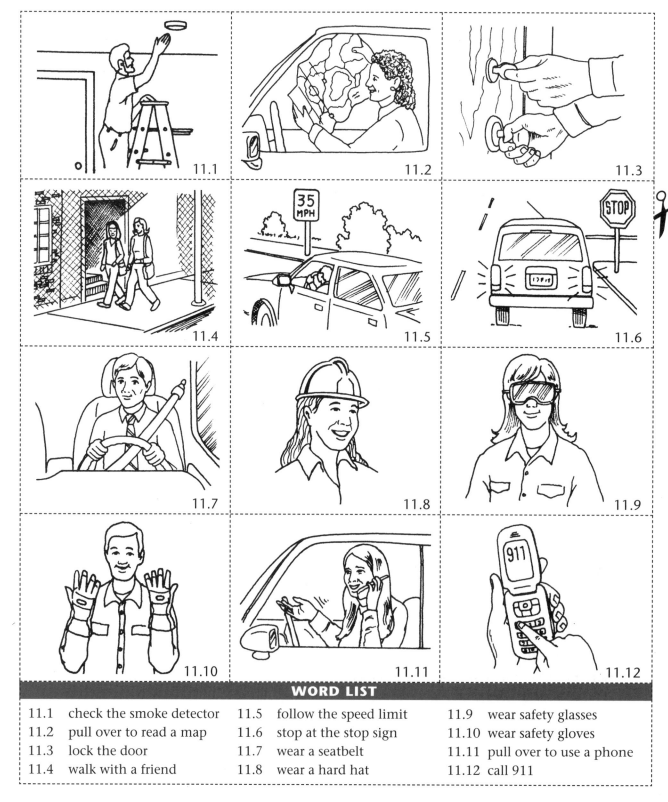

WORD LIST		
11.1 check the smoke detector	11.5 follow the speed limit	11.9 wear safety glasses
11.2 pull over to read a map	11.6 stop at the stop sign	11.10 wear safety gloves
11.3 lock the door	11.7 wear a seatbelt	11.11 pull over to use a phone
11.4 walk with a friend	11.8 wear a hard hat	11.12 call 911

Grid Game

1. Cut apart the picture cards from page 124.

2. Work with a partner. Don't show your paper to your partner.

Partner A: Put a picture on a square on the grid. Use the picture and the person or people in the square to make a sentence. Tell your partner the sentence: *You should stop at the stop sign.*

Partner B: Listen to your partner. Put your picture on the person that Partner A says. Check what you hear: *Should what?*

3. When your grids are full, look at them. Are they the same?
Yes: change roles. No: try again.

I	You	She
He	They	My partner
The driver	The student	The factory worker
The teacher	The manager	My coworker

Sentence Maker

1. Work with a group of 3 or 4 students. Cut apart the cards.
2. Choose a Recorder.
3. Use the word cards to make 10 different sentences or questions in 10 minutes.
   The Recorder writes the group's sentences and questions.

I	YOU	SHE	HE
WE	THEY	SHOULD	SHOULDN'T
WEAR	A	SEATBELT	SAFETY
GLOVES	BOOTS	GLASSES	BE
CAREFUL	CARELESS	.	?

Unit 12 Free Time

Let's Go to the Beach

1. Work with 3 classmates.

2. Label what you see in the picture.

3. Check your spelling in a dictionary.

go to the beach

KEEP GOING!

Talk about different activities for different kinds of weather. What things do you like to do?

Take Me Out to the Ball Game

1. Work with a partner. Look at the pictures. Match the sentences to the pictures.

2. **Partner A:** Say the sentences.

  Partner B: Act out the sentences. Use actions and words.

3. Change roles.

_____ Find your seat and sit down.

_____ Buy a ticket at the ticket window.

_____ Eat your snacks and watch the game.

_1_ Look out the window. It's a great day for a baseball game!

_____ Take a bus to the stadium.

_____ Walk to the ticket window.

_____ You're hungry. Buy some snacks.

_____ Give your ticket to the person at the entrance.

KEEP GOING!

Work in a group. Take turns. Act out the sentences. Say what your classmate is doing.

We're Going to Have a Great Time!

Partner A
• **Read a sentence to Partner B.** • **Answer Partner B's question.** • **Watch Partner B write.**
1. It's going to be sunny tomorrow. 2. I'm going to go to the park with my friends. 3. We're going to play soccer. 4. It's going to be a lot of fun.
• **Listen to Partner B.** • **Check what you hear. Say: *Going to what?*** • **Write the sentence.**
5.
6.
7.
8.

- FOLD HERE -

Partner B
• **Listen to Partner A.** • **Check what you hear. Say: *Going to what?*** • **Write the sentence.**
1.
2.
3.
4.
• **Read a sentence to Partner A.** • **Answer Partner A's question.** • **Watch Partner A write.**
5. I'm going to see my friend this weekend. 6. I'm going to take the bus. 7. We're going to go out to eat. 8. We're going to have a great time!

KEEP GOING!
Write 4 sentences about different things you or someone else is going to do.
Talk about your sentences with your class.
We're going to buy a new car.

How Much Are the Tickets?

1. Work with 2 classmates. Say all the lines in the script.

2. Choose your character.

3. Finish the conversation. Write more lines for each character.

4. Practice the lines.

5. Act out the role-play with your group.

Scene	Characters	Props
A living room	• Friend 1 • Friend 2 • Friend 3	A newspaper

The Script

Friend 1: What are we going to do this Saturday?

Friend 2: I want to see a movie. What do you want to do?

Friend 3: I don't want to see a movie. We always go to the movies.

Friend 1: What should we do?

Friend 3: We should go see Black Cat. Their music is great.

Friend 2: Where are they playing?

Friend 3: They're at the Hard Hat Theater.

Friend 1: How much are the tickets?

KEEP GOING!

Watch your classmates' role-plays. Write the answers to these questions:
How much are Black Cat tickets? Where do the friends go?

Greetings to You

1. Read the survey questions. Mark your answers with a check (✓).

2. Interview 3–9 classmates. Mark your classmates' answers.

Do you buy greeting cards for _____?	My Answers	My Classmates' Answers								
		1	2	3	4	5	6	7	8	9
holidays										
birthdays										
Valentine's Day										
Christmas										
other special occasions										

3. Use the chart above to complete the bar graph.

Number of Classmates					
10					
9					
8					
7					
6					
5					
4					
3					
2					
1					
	holidays	birthdays	Valentine's Day	Christmas	other special occasions

KEEP GOING!

Discuss this information with your class. Write 5 sentences.

3 students buy greeting cards for Valentine's Day.

Lots of Fun for Little Money

The Project: Make a brochure of inexpensive ways to have fun in the different seasons
Materials: blank paper, scissors, magazines, tape or glue, and markers

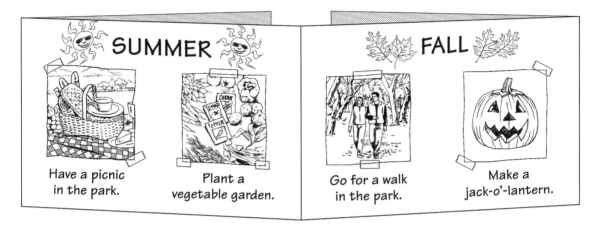

SUMMER

Have a picnic
in the park.

Plant a
vegetable garden.

FALL

Go for a walk
in the park.

Make a
jack-o'-lantern.

1. Work with 4–5 students. Introduce yourself.

2. Choose your job.

> **Leader:** Help your group work together.
> **Timekeeper:** Watch the time.
> **Recorder:** Write the team's ideas.
> **Reporter:** Tell the class about the project.
> **Supplier:** Get the supplies.

3. Talk about the answers to this question: What are some easy, inexpensive ways
   to have fun in the different seasons?

> **Timekeeper:** Give the team 5 minutes.
> **Leader:** Ask each person the question.
> **Recorder:** Write the seasons and the different activities for each season.

4. Make the brochure.

> **Supplier:** Get the supplies from your teacher.
> **Team:** Create the brochure.
> • Fold the paper into four equal sections to make a brochure.
> • Write the name of a different season on each section of the brochure.
> • Draw (or cut out and glue) pictures of seasonal activities under the correct seasons.
> • Write about each activity.

5. Share your brochure with the class.

> **Reporter:** Talk about the brochure and different activities that people
> can do in the different seasons.
> *In the winter when it's cold, you can stay at home and make cookies and watch a video.*

KEEP GOING!
Vote on which group has the best activities.

Picture Cards

1. Cut apart the picture cards. Use the word list to write the words on the back.
2. Work with a partner.
   Partner A: Show the picture card to your partner.
   Partner B: Say the words.
3. Change roles.

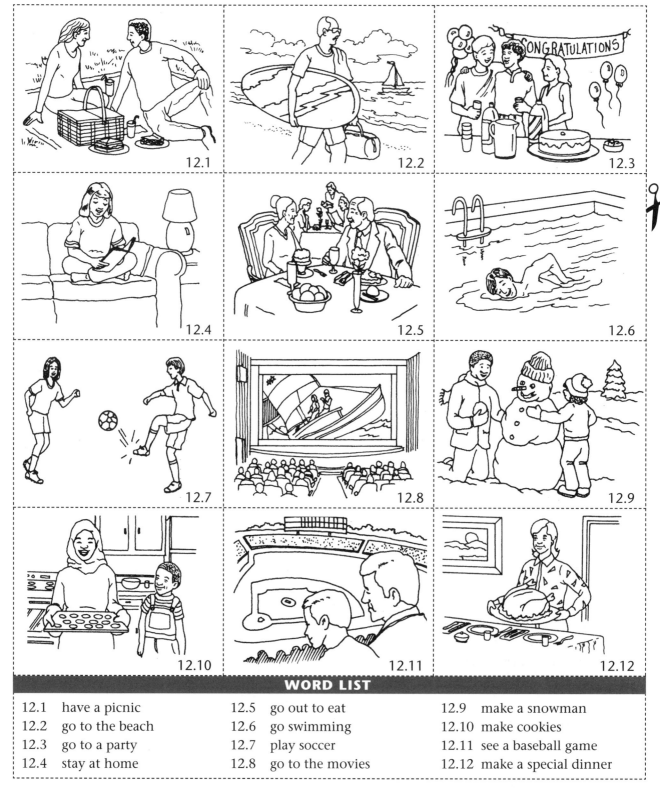

WORD LIST		
12.1 have a picnic	12.5 go out to eat	12.9 make a snowman
12.2 go to the beach	12.6 go swimming	12.10 make cookies
12.3 go to a party	12.7 play soccer	12.11 see a baseball game
12.4 stay at home	12.8 go to the movies	12.12 make a special dinner

Grid Game

1. Cut apart the picture cards from page 134.
2. Work with a partner. Don't show your paper to your partner.
   Partner A: Put a picture on a square on the grid. Use the picture and the month in the square to make a sentence. Tell your partner the sentence: *He's going to go to the beach in July.*
   Partner B: Listen to your partner. Put your picture on the month that Partner A says.
   Check what you hear: *Going to what?*
3. When your grids are full, look at them. Are they the same?
   Yes: change roles. No: try again.

January	February	March
April	May	June
July	August	September
October	November	December

Sentence Maker

1. Work with a group of 3 or 4 students. Cut apart the cards.

2. Choose a Recorder.

3. Use the word cards to make 10 different sentences or questions in 10 minutes.
The Recorder writes the group's sentences and questions.

I	YOU	HE	SHE
IT	AM	ARE	IS
GOING	TO	BE	NOT
WORK	HAVE	FUN	TOMORROW
SUNNY	CLOUDY	.	?